THE PRACTICAL GUIDE TO HR ANALYTICS

THE PRACTICAL GUIDE TO HR ANALYTICS

Using Data to Inform, Transform, and Empower HR Decisions

Shonna D. Waters,
Valerie N. Streets,
Lindsay McFarlane, and
Rachael Johnson-Murray

Society for Human Resource Management
Alexandria, Virginia I shrm.org

Society for Human Resource Management, India Office
Mumbai, India I shrmindia.org

Society for Human Resource Management
Haidian District Beijing, China I shrm.org/cn

Society for Human Resource Management, Middle East and Africa Office
Dubai, UAE I shrm.org/pages/mena.aspx

SOCIETY FOR HUMAN
RESOURCE MANAGEMENT

This publication is designed to provide accurate and authoritative information regarding the subject matter covered. It is sold with the understanding that neither the publisher nor the author is engaged in rendering legal or other professional service. If legal advice or other expert assistance is required, the services of a competent, licensed professional should be sought. The federal and state laws discussed in this book are subject to frequent revision and interpretation by amendments or judicial revisions that may significantly affect employer or employee rights and obligations. Readers are encouraged to seek legal counsel regarding specific policies and practices in their organizations.

This book is published by the Society for Human Resource Management (SHRM). The interpretations, conclusions, and recommendations in this book are those of the author and do not necessarily represent those of the publisher.

This publication may not be reproduced, stored in a retrieval system, or transmitted in whole or in part, in any form or by any means, electronic, mechanical, photocopying, recording, or otherwise, without the prior written permission of the publisher, or authorization through payment of the appropriate per-copy fee to the Copyright Clearance Center, Inc., 222 Rosewood Drive, Danvers, MA 01923, 978-750-8600, fax 978-646-8600, or on the Web at www.copyright. com. Requests to the publisher for permission should be addressed to SHRM Book Permissions, 1800 Duke Street, Alexandria, VA 22314, or online at http://www.shrm.org/about-shrm/pages/copyright--permissions.aspx.

SHRM books and products are available on most online bookstores and through the SHRMStore at www.shrmstore.org.

The Society for Human Resource Management (SHRM) is the world's largest HR professional society, represent-ing 285,000 members in more than 165 countries. For nearly seven decades, the Society has been the leading provider of resources serving the needs of HR professionals and advancing the practice of human resource management. SHRM has more than 575 affiliated chapters within the United States and subsidiary offices in China, India and United Arab Emirates. Visit us at shrm.org.

Library of Congress Cataloging-in-Publication Data has been applied for and is on file with the Library of Congress. ISBN (pbk): 978-1-586-44532-4; ISBN (PDF): 978-1-586-44533-1; ISBN (EPUB): 978-1-586-44534-8; ISBN (MOBI): 978-1-586-44535-5

Printed in the United States of America

FIRST EDITION

PB Printing   10 9 8 7 6 5 4 3 2 1   61.15020 | 18-0267

I'd like to dedicate this book to the many amazing teachers and mentors throughout my career who taught me how to use science and analytics to solve business challenges. To my constant sources of inspiration, Scarlett and Emeline. I am in awe of your endless energy, playfulness, and unconditional love.

—Shonna

To those who are terrified of analytics. I'm proud of you for picking up this book. You are an inspiration. Be kind to yourself in the learning process.

—Lindsay

Table of Contents

List of Tables, Figures, and Case Studies

Tables

Figures

Cases

Preface

Seventh-grade algebra was the first time I received a C in a class. From that point on, I began telling myself a story: I hated math. I wasn't good at it. I could manage without it because I was going to be a scientist, not a mathematician. Problem solved, right? As you might expect, I couldn't escape algebra quite that easily. I had to face my fears in college when I took my first statistics class. I spent a few weeks with that same seventh-grade feeling in the pit of my stomach before I finally decided to reach out for some tutoring.

We had talked about the normal curve for two weeks when suddenly the light bulb went on. Things started making sense. From that moment, statistics became different. It wasn't math. We weren't talking about computing the height of anonymous buildings. I was learning that I could use statistics to address problems that were much more meaningful to me—increasing student learning, selecting high performers, learning what makes a better team, and so on. Even more unexpectedly, my appreciation for statistics made me like algebra.

I spent much of the first part of my career using analytics to help organizations make better hiring and promotion decisions, as well as predicting and reducing turnover. In more recent years, I've used analytics to help leaders evaluate and reform a wide range of programs, including selection, compensation, recruitment, training and development, performance management, and rewards and recognition. In my current role, I apply analytics to better understand how to create lasting behavior change and evaluate the impact of large-scale coaching programs. Through those experiences, I have seen firsthand the impact that analytics can have on both the credibility of the HR function and business outcomes.

Although I have long loved analytics and the value they can bring, I didn't see writing a book about them in my future. During my time as SHRM's vice president of research, I was asked to develop a seminar on HR analytics. I had the opportunity to present that seminar to a handful of audiences across the country. I arrived early to set up and introduce myself to attendees as they entered the room, and I often asked why they were there. Over and over again, I heard responses with a similar theme—"I know this is important, but I'm not sure where to start."

Many HR professionals get into the field in unexpected ways, but a common draw is our love of people and desire to make their experience better at work. Our field has evolved a great deal and continues to evolve. Expectations in large organizations have changed. The availability of data and the expectation that it will be used to ground decision-making is no longer limited to other business functions. Classes on human-capital analytics and research methods are now core parts of degree programs in human resources.

This book was written for those of us living in the transition. Whether you are an HR leader or an HR generalist needing to navigate analytics rather than specialize in them, or early in your career and trying to decide if an analytics specialization is the right path, this book was written for you. This isn't a textbook or an analytics handbook. It won't teach you big data techniques or discriminant analysis. What it will do is help you get started and give you some options where to go next.

Developing comfort and fluency with analytics can empower you not just to create new knowledge about what's going on within your organizational walls, but also to be better equipped to bring in knowledge from the outside. If nothing else, HR professionals need to become savvy consumers of analytics to distinguish between fads and robust findings when making decisions.

When we started writing this book, we began by developing an outline that covered everything we thought was important, with statistical principles and theory, and highly detailed and technical information. We ended up with a very comprehensive, very *boring* book outline. We weren't excited about writing it, and we certainly couldn't imagine that you would be excited about reading it. So, we scrapped the whole thing and started over.

Where we ended up was an approach that attempts to put analytics in context. We introduce you to Jen, an HR director confronted with a common problem that bubbled up from the business: turnover of critical talent. You get to follow Jen's story from problem diagnosis to the proposed solution, with breaks in the story for teaching content and space for your own reflection. We also provide a set of appendices designed to help you apply the content to your own story within your organizational context.

HR professionals are a diverse bunch, so we built features into this book to give you options to tailor the content to meet your individual needs. We provide opportunities to dive deeper into the topics that interest you through callouts to curated resources throughout. Each chapter has a section called "From the SHRM Research Lab" that integrates a little bit of behavioral science and research. We include a few sections on how things might look different in small organizations. In the end, we hope our use of variety, story, and application come together to provide an approachable resource for a topic that can seem less than warm.

—Shonna Waters

Acknowledgments

Although four of us are on the byline, we would like to thank the many others who made integral contributions to this book. First is Dr. Scott Oppler, who diligently reviewed nearly every word from his other office at Panera Bread. We were honored to have someone with such a distinguished career in measurement and analytics as a mentor for this effort, and our readers will undoubtedly benefit from his involvement. We included a range of case studies in the book to provide you with examples of the wide range of analytics applications. That content would not have been possible without our generous and innovative partners: Dr. Rich Cober at MicroStrategy, Marc Bishop and Kasey Fleisher Hickey at BetterUp, Dr. Joy Oliver at Management Concepts, Dr. Matt Fleisher at FTI Consulting, Kathy Stewart at US Customs and Border Protection, Rachel Callan at Liberty Mutual, Kristie Buys at Veterinary Holistic Care, Paula Traugh at Hilton, and Patrick Carey at Pratt and Whitney. Montrese Hamilton helped us obtain necessary permissions for content throughout the book.

Author Biographies

Shonna D. Waters

Dr. Shonna Waters is a regional vice president of behavioral science at BetterUp, where she leads a team that conducts research to advance the science of behavior change and consults with organizations to apply it in support of business goals. Prior to joining BetterUp, she was the vice president of research at the Society for Human Resource Management (SHRM). She has spent her professional career helping organizations use analytics to improve performance and the employee experience. Dr. Waters spent over fifteen years as an external and internal consultant applying analytics to a wide range of human-capital challenges. While at the National Security Agency (NSA), she led the transformation of NSA's promotion, performance management, and awards and recognition systems; the design and validation of NSA's analyst hiring assessments; and a variety of other evaluation and organizational performance projects. Dr. Waters holds a PhD in industrial-organizational (I-O) psychology and statistics and a certificate in leadership coaching from Georgetown University. She is also an Associate Certified Coach (ACC) through the International Coach Federation (ICF), and a SHRM Senior Certified Professional (SHRM-SCP). She is currently a professor in Georgetown University's School of Continuing Studies and previously taught statistics and research methods at the George Washington University and the University of Minnesota. Her work has been published in a variety of peer-reviewed journals and books, and she has published over fifty technical reports and presented at more than twenty-five professional conferences.

Valerie N. Streets

Dr. Valerie Streets is a quantitative research consultant at CEB, now Gartner, where she uses data analytics to provide businesses with insights and recommendations. Prior to that, Dr. Streets was the first postdoctoral research fellow at SHRM. In that role, she worked to expand SHRM's thought leadership by disseminating her findings to the HR and academic communities via conference presentations, publications, toolkits, magazine and blog articles, and effective practice guides. Before joining SHRM, she worked as a researcher and adjunct professor at the University of Tulsa. She has ten years of research experience and three years of experience as an independent consultant. Her research specialties include talent acquisition and diversity and inclusion. She holds a PhD in I-O psychology from Old Dominion University. She has taught courses in statistics, research methods, I-O psychology, and organizational behavior at the University of Tulsa, Old Dominion University, and Virginia Wesleyan College. Her work has been published in several peer-reviewed journals and books and she has presented at fifteen professional conferences.

Lindsay McFarlane

Lindsay McFarlane works for the Federal Emergency Management Agency (FEMA) where she develops and validates competency models and assessments, and supports the learning and development strategy of FEMA management and employees. Prior to that, she was the senior specialist of strategic research initiatives at SHRM where she led large research projects to support the organization's key strategic initiatives, including the development of talent analytics tools for the HR profession, competency-based products and resources, and certification exams. In her career at SHRM, Ms. McFarlane contributed to the development of the Competency Development Plan, Competency Diagnostic Tools, and the book *Defining HR Success: 9 Critical Competencies for HR Professionals* (2015). She wrote for the SHRM certification newsletter and has been published in HR Magazine. Ms. McFarlane is skilled in qualitative and quantitative organizational research, data analysis, competency modeling, project management, training, and instructional systems development.

Ms. McFarlane earned a bachelor's in psychology from Virginia Tech and a master's in I-O psychology from the University of Maryland, Baltimore County, and she is a SHRM Senior Certified Professional (SHRM-SCP). She is an active member of the Society for Industrial and Organizational Psychology (SIOP), Personnel Testing Council Metropolitan Washington (PTCMW), and International Personnel Assessment Council (IPAC), and volunteers in her local community.

Rachael Johnson-Murray

Rachael Johnson-Murray is the manager of research translation at the Society for Human Resource Management (SHRM). She contributes to the creation of research-based content for HR professionals to use in an applied setting. At SHRM, Rachael uses data visualization and communication techniques to bridge the gap between HR practices and scientific research. Prior to joining SHRM, she spent seven years helping organizations develop and establish HRIS and analytics capabilities. Her work allowed these organizations to extract stories from their data. She was most recently the senior HRIS analyst at Total Wine and More. In that role she led data integrity and systems integration initiatives, standardized business processes, established HR metrics and reports, conducted organizational assessments, and piloted initiatives to further support the organization's business goals. Rachael earned her bachelor's in psychology from Minnesota State University at Mankato, and her master's in I-O psychology from the University of Tennessee at Chattanooga.

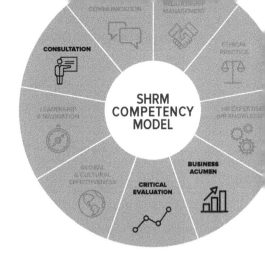

1

Define the Business Challenge

Chapter Snapshot

Questions we will answer:

- What are HR analytics?
- Why are they important?
- Why should I read this book and what can I expect?

....

Meet Jen. She's the HR director of a 1,200-person company. What started as rumblings of an issue has become a full-blown problem. A few vocal managers have been complaining that her company is struggling with turnover. She doesn't know how serious the issue is. She does know that the HR department can't be perceived as unresponsive.

....

HR has a tough job. It has to serve employees; protect the business; keep up with ever-changing laws and regulations at local, state, and federal levels; and figure out how to do more with less, faster. These demands leave HR professionals with big questions: How can we make better decisions about where to invest our limited resources? How can we deliver solutions that make employees happy? How can we convince the C-suite to invest in people initiatives? How can we make sure HR helps the organization achieve business outcomes?

HR analytics can help with all of these things and more. It's not a silver bullet, but it is a powerful tool for elevating the credibility of the HR function.

I know—I've described only the tip of the iceberg of what makes your job hard. Now I'm saying you need to learn something that might be new. It may also be intimidating. You might have even gone into HR to avoid having to take extra math classes. But hang in there. I'm going to make this as painless as possible.

In this book, I'll use an example of a common, real-life business challenge to teach you basic concepts. This example will help you understand how to

- identify where analytics can help,
- differentiate types of metrics and analytics,
- use different types of metrics and analytics, and
- maximize their impact.

This book provides an approachable introduction to HR analytics. I won't get into the technical details of building databases or cleaning and analyzing data. Instead, I'll give you enough information to know what to request from an analyst and what to do with those results. But don't worry—if you want to dig deeper, I'll direct you to other resources to get you started.

Throughout this book, you'll notice some icons that keep popping up. These indicate opportunities to get into something extra. Anytime you see "Take a Deeper Dive," I have curated outside resources, giving you the option to go more in-depth. As an HR professional, you know that "telling ain't training." To that end, I've built in reflection questions and activities throughout to make sure you're absorbing everything. Wherever you see "Reflection," it'll be your turn to assess the situation and share your thoughts. There's also a whole workbook in the appendices to help you apply the content back at the office. Lastly, each chapter ends with insights from the SHRM Research Lab. Consider this optional information if you'd really like to dive into a certain topic.

There you'll see research findings from the behavioral sciences to explain why things happen. Now that you know how to use this book, let's dig in!

> **Reflection**
>
> Let's return to Jen's situation. Her plate is full. How might she go about deciding how big of a priority the managers' complaints are?
>
> _____
>
> _____
>
> _____
>
> _____
>
> _____

....

Jen knows these managers are usually pretty quick to complain. However, she wants to be responsive. She decides to take a look at some metrics. She asks an analyst to pull the last year's turnover numbers. They indicate turnover increased about a percentage point over the last four quarters. Jen doesn't see a problem, so she writes a polite email to the managers and moves onto the next item on her list.

The next day Jen is called into an emergency meeting. She walks into the room and sees her boss sitting there along with Mark, the director of the managers who complained to her yesterday. No one looks happy. She senses that she's in the hot seat.

Mark asks Jen to explain what happened. Suddenly she's getting peppered with questions. How is it possible that turnover isn't a problem? All of Mark's direct reports claim to be losing their best people. What is the company's turnover rate? Is that high or low? What if only the best performers are leaving?

Ultimately, Mark says he doesn't care what the numbers say. They can't meet their objectives without the necessary talent and that is her problem to fix.

After the meeting, Jen's boss sticks around to talk to her. She starts by asking Jen to reflect.

....

Reflection

What went wrong in Jen's situation? How might this all have been avoided?

_____

_____

_____

_____

_____

In the past, HR professionals typically relied on their understanding of HR processes and the organization to make decisions and serve their stakeholders. Hard data were limited. Any data that were captured were done so manually or were housed in different systems that didn't talk to each other.

Luckily, the world is changing. Thanks to advancing technology, data and information are everywhere, which means they're easily and quickly accessible. Most organizations have human resource information systems (HRISs) to record basic transactions, such as hiring date, compensation, promotions, and performance ratings. Increasingly, organizations are also collecting information about the learning and development of their employees. This includes proficiency levels of various skills and aptitudes, as well as training and development engagements and outcomes, such as end-of-training scores.

Despite having access to more data and analytic power than ever before, many HR organizations still aren't relying on those to make significant decisions. Finance, customer service, marketing, and sales functions all use data extensively. Your stakeholders are using data and analytics more and more. Their expectations and recognition of the importance of talent-related data are increasing too. Not only are your managers and directors concerned about something they see as a big business problem, they may also be expecting you to approach it the same way they approach issues in their department. For HR leaders to have broader organizational impact, they too need to shift from a focus on HR processes to the impact of talent on the broader business strategy and outcomes.

··

Jen took the first logical step in looking into her company's turnover rate, but what did she miss by stopping there?

To start, organizations act more like complex ecosystems than as single organisms. Looking at only the top level or company-wide turnover rate, Jen may miss what's happening in a specific skill area or part of the company. She also may not have enough information to understand who is leaving and what impact those departures have on the business. If the bulk of the work is being accomplished by a handful of star employees, the impact may be a lot higher than the numbers alone reveal. The managers may be sensing something that hasn't yet started showing up in the metrics HR routinely analyzes. Jen may need to collect more information to fully understand the situation.

Maybe Jen has just fallen into old habits. She had a transactional interaction with the managers. They complained. Jen did research. She sent them the outcome. Today's HR professionals have to move from transacting to consulting. The managers are the ones closest to the people and business issues. Jen can partner with them; she'll bring her knowledge and skills together with theirs to understand the situation and co-create a solution.

··

There's a lot of talk about big data, algorithms, and automation. However, the value of data is limited by your ability to extract information and insights from them. Organizations are using technology to collect more and more data. They need people capable of interpreting the data and extracting valuable information from them. Equally important, they must help turn that information into insights that can be used to make better decisions and provide a competitive advantage.

Analytics provides a way to demonstrate the linkage between people and business outcomes. HR analytics (also called people analytics or talent analytics) use measurement and analysis techniques to understand, improve, and optimize the people side of business.[1] Data are the raw numbers you track. When an employee who reports to one of the managers in Jen's scenario leaves, it creates data. Metrics focus on counting, tracking, and presenting past data. Analytics uses statistics to help you see patterns in the data. Figure 1.1 shows how these three pieces lead to HR solutions.

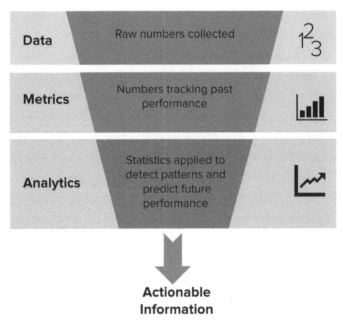

Figure 1.1. Analytics process

Jen was looking at the complaint through a metrics lens. How many people have left, and has that number increased over time? Shifting her lens to analytics—focusing on who is leaving, what is their impact on the business, and why are they leaving—can give Jen a lot more information.

Take a Deeper Dive

For more on differentiating between data and metrics, see "Know the Difference between Your Data and Your Metrics" by Jeff Bladt and Bob Filbin.[2]

Survey evidence shows that HR's credibility increases as it starts using data to inform its decisions.[3] This means that not only can analytics help you diagnose and solve problems, it also can make you look good, make the HR function look good, and positively impact the bottom line.

....

Jen and her boss talk through what went wrong. This officially becomes Jen's top priority until she comes to a resolution that the managers are on board with.

....

In the next chapter, I'll help you understand what you'll need to use analytics. I'll also help you figure out what you already have.

How Might This Look Different in Small Organizations?

The example we're working through uses a large organization as the backdrop. However, things might look different in small organizations. For starters, you have fewer employees. Even one person leaving could significantly impact your turnover rate. This means you may need to rely even more heavily on qualitative information (things like interviews with stakeholders or employee exit interviews) and external information (market conditions such as unemployment rate, external benchmarks, etc.). Later, we'll revisit how Jen's situation might unfold in a small organization.

 From the SHRM Research Lab

People aren't as good at making decisions as they think.[4] We like to think of ourselves as rational actors, but our informational-processing limitations, emotions, and biases get in our way. The world is complex and humans have developed ways to help simplify it. So-called cognitive biases are ways our brains help us take shortcuts to deal with four primary problems: information overload, lack of meaning, the need to act fast, and knowing what needs to be remembered for later.[5]

These shortcuts come at a cost. There are also four primary problems that these solutions create: we don't see everything, we create illusions, our quick decisions can be seriously flawed, and our memories can reinforce those errors. Despite all the evidence that our judgments are faulty, leaders typically rely on their guts.[6]

 Take a Deeper Dive

For more detail on cognitive biases, see Figure 1.2.

We can do better. There are ways to mitigate the limitations in our decision-making, including relying more heavily on the systematic collection, analysis, and combination of data. Professional judgment that incorporates hard data or is based on statistical models is more accurate than judgment based on individual experience.[7] Information based on scientific research is more accurate than the opinions of experts.[8] This means that if you start using analytics, not only can you improve your decisions, you can also help your leaders make better decisions. This is a win-win situation.

If we can make better decisions, why do so many leaders still rely on gut instincts? Unfortunately, people tend to trust their own judgment more than data and algorithms, even when they know it is less accurate.[9] We call this "algorithm aversion."[10] Although it can make prediction worse,[11] people are more willing to trust algorithms if they can insert their own judgment by tweaking the outcome.

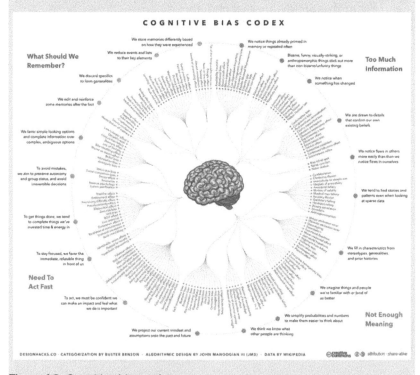

Figure 1.2. Cognitive bias codex

Key Takeaways

- HR analytics apply measurement and statistical techniques to identify and understand patterns in data. This information helps optimize the people side of the business.
- HR analytics can improve the credibility of the HR function by showing the linkage between people and business outcomes.
- Technological advancements have made data—about people, processes, business outcomes, customer engagement, and more—available. Other fields are using these data to build a competitive advantage, and they are expecting you to do it too.

Pratt & Whitney Creates a Workforce-Planning Vision

The People Analytics (PA) team at Pratt & Whitney was early into the development of an analytics function when they realized that sophisticated data models weren't going to win over their stakeholders. When tasked with creating a workforce-planning portfolio that applied across the organization, the PA team readied themselves to take on a long-tailed and ever-evolving data project. At the onset of the project, they found that each stakeholder group described the workforce-planning process differently. This made proving the value of the new function an uphill battle.

The PA team began with the critical step of understanding the anticipated project outcomes by holding informal meetings to collect input from each stakeholder group. Using clear and concise language, they defined an overarching value proposition that fit the needs of all stakeholders: workforce planning provides Pratt & Whitney with the ability to place the right people with the right skills in the right roles at the right time through agile planning tools and methods. Pratt & Whitney took the additional step of literally visualizing the more popular inputs and outputs of its models to show all stakeholders that their variables would be considered (see Figure 1.3).

This visual allowed all customers, whether mathematical gurus or relative newcomers to data, to clearly understand and reference the workforce-planning vision.

Even with the stakeholders on board and the anticipated outcomes defined, the PA team encountered challenges. They concluded that no single model could answer every stakeholder's workforce-planning questions. They quickly discovered that it was the ability to deliver quick wins from many imperfect analytic models that allowed for healthy dialogue and helped guide the workforce-planning scope in a way that always pointed back to the value proposition. The solution was to adopt an agile approach to workforce planning: the components of each model would vary based on the stakeholder group and the specific workforce-planning questions that the group was trying to answer (Table 1.1).

Despite the ever-changing nature of stakeholder needs and countless additions to the workforce-planning portfolio, it was not long before the PA team offered insights to the business that began to drive meaningful decisions that in turn became points of maturation in the workforce-planning portfolio.

Through this iterative process, Pratt & Whitney continuously improves upon its interconnected workforce-planning toolkit through connections between HR strategy and the larger business plan. By ensuring a collective understanding of the initiative's output at the onset of the process, the PA team ensured that analytic projects gained buy-in and became an integrated part in a proactive HR decision-making process.

Figure 1.3. Workforce-planning vision

Table 1.1. Example models

Model Description	Model Components	Dialogue Assessing Model Components
Internal Labor Market (ILM) Mapping	Potential + Performance + Attrition	Does the company have an attrition issue for high potentials or performers? What does a healthy talent pool look like? What might we do to incentivize high potentials or performers to stay with us for longer?
Predictive Attrition and Survival Analysis	Demographics + Retention	Do we have a healthy amount of retention? Do we have any retirement bubbles on the horizon? Is there an opportunity to improve on diversity representation?
Capacity Planning Collaborations	Competencies + Location	Could a skills shortage in a plant lead to production delays? Where are the best regions to recruit particular skill sets?

Endnotes

1. Wendy Wang-Audia, *Talent Analytics: From Small Data to Big Data*, research bulletin (Bersin by Deloitte, 2013).

2. Jeff Bladt and Bob Filbin, "Know the Difference between Your Data and Your Metrics," *Harvard Business Review* 4 (2013), https://hbr.org/2013/03/know-the-difference-between-yo.

3. Economist Intelligence Unit, *Use of Workforce Analytics for Competitive Advantage* (Alexandria, VA: Society for Human Resource Management, 2016).

4. Daniel Kahneman and Amos Tversky, "Prospect Theory: An Analysis of Decision under Risk," *Econometrica* 47 (1979): 263–91; and Paul E. Meehl, *Clinical versus Statistical Prediction: A Theoretical Analysis and a Review of the Evidence* (Minneapolis: University of Minnesota Press, 1954).

5. Buster Benson, "Cognitive Bias Cheat Sheet," *Better Humans* (blog), September 1, 2016, https://betterhumans.coach.me/cognitive-bias-cheat-sheet-55a472476b18.

6. Economist Intelligence Unit, *Gut and Gigabytes: Capitalising on the Art and Science in Decision Making* (London: PwC, 2014), https://www.pwc.com/gx/en/issues/data-and-analytics/big-decisions-survey/assets/big-decisions2014.pdf;

and Jenna Filipkowski, *Insightful HR: Integrating Quality Data for Better Talent Decisions*, white paper, Human Capital Institute Research, April 28, 2015, http://pcdn4.hci.org/files/field_content_file/2015%20Oracle.pdf.

7. Ian Ayres, *Super Crunchers: Why Thinking-by-Numbers Is the New Way to Be Smart* (New York: Bantam Books, 2008); Howard N. Garb and William M. Grove, "On the Merits of Clinical Judgment: Comment," *American Psychologist* 60, no. 6 (2005): 658–659; and Colin Lewis-Beck and Michael Lewis-Beck, *Applied Regression: An Introduction*, 2nd ed. (Newbury Park, CA: Sage Publications, 2016).

8. Elliott M. Antman et al., "A Comparison of Results of Meta-analyses of Randomized Control Trials and Recommendations of Clinical Experts: Treatments for Myocardial Infarction," *Journal of the American Medical Association* 268, no. 2 (1992): 240–48.

9. Berkeley J. Dietvorst, Joseph P. Simmons, and Cade Massey, "Overcoming Algorithm Aversion: People Will Use Imperfect Algorithms If They Can (Even Slightly) Modify Them," *Management Science Articles in Advance*, November 4, 2016, https://doi.org/10.1287/mnsc.2016.2643.

10. Walter Frick, "Here's Why People Trust Human Judgment over Algorithms," *Harvard Business Review*, February 27, 2015, https://hbr.org/2015/02/heres-why-people-trust-human-judgment-over-algorithms.

11. Meehl, *Clinical versus Statistical Prediction*.

2

Understand the Analytics Domain

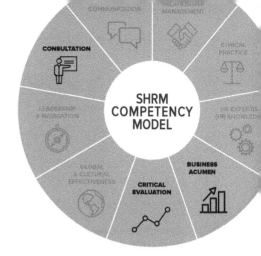

SHRM COMPETENCY MODEL

COMMUNICATION · RELATIONSHIP MANAGEMENT · ETHICAL PRACTICE · HR EXPERTISE (HR KNOWLEDGE) · BUSINESS ACUMEN · CRITICAL EVALUATION · GLOBAL & CULTURAL EFFECTIVENESS · LEADERSHIP & NAVIGATION · CONSULTATION

 Chapter Snapshot

Questions we will answer:

- How do I respond to any pressure I'm feeling to resolve the people problem my business leaders are complaining about?
- How can I build a stronger partnership with business leaders?
- What skills do I need to have to develop my expertise in HR analytics?

....

After some creative calendar clearing, Jen sits down to wrestle with her new top priority. The managers are acting like there is a talent emergency. She doesn't see evidence of a turnover problem—at least based on company-wide metrics. Regardless, it's clear that this issue isn't going away, so it's time to dig in.

Jen decides to schedule a meeting with the managers who first raised the turnover concerns. But first she wants to make sure she's done her homework. She needs to turn this relationship around fast. She already has the organization-wide turnover numbers and percentages over the last year broken down by quarter (see Table 2.1). Turnover did go up, but by just over a percentage point. It's no big deal, right?

....

Table 2.1. Turnover metrics from the last year

Acme Corporation Turnover 2017

Metrics	Q1	Q2	Q3	Q4	2017 Average
Separations	197	197	201	209	201
Average Headcount	1,227	1,214	1,199	1,208	1,212
Turnover Rate	16.06%	16.23%	16.76%	17.30%	16.58%

Note: Total number of employees varies due to ongoing replacements.

So, is a 1.24 percent increase in turnover a big deal? Maybe, but maybe not: it's all relative. With an organization-wide turnover rate of 6 percent, an increase of close to a percentage point may be nothing to sneeze at. An additional fifteen people walked out the door as a result of that approximately 1 percent increase. To get a better sense of what might be going on, Jen may need more information to better assess what she's seeing.

What's going on here? The managers are sensing a problem. As the HR director, Jen is trying to be objective and evidence based. She wants to use data to help guide her decision-making. The problem is that numbers don't often tell the whole story and they're only as good as their interpretation. That's why analytics has become so important in organizations.

Reflection

What questions might you ask to help determine whether turnover is a problem? Is a 1 percent increase large or small? What kind of data and metrics do you use in your organization?

_____

_____

_____

_____

_____

_____

_____

_____

_____

Answering some of the following questions would provide additional context to help evaluate the organizational data Jen has on hand:

- Is the increase she's seeing within the normal fluctuations in turnover from the organization?
- Are there seasonal or shock effects (e.g., events such as bonuses, raises, or promotions) that would explain this year's pattern?
- What's typical right now for companies like Jen's in the market?
- Is there anything happening outside the company that might impact turnover now or in the future?
- Is the departmental turnover for these managers higher than the company's average?

Notice that these questions require looking both within and outside the organization to evaluate the forces that could be impacting the labor pool. Sometimes they can even interact. For example, it's common to see a spike in turnover after a promotion cycle. Some people will leave because they're upset and feel passed over for a promotion, while others might leave because they're now more competitive for other jobs after receiving a promotion. However, people may be less likely to leave if unemployment is high. That's why developing a strong understanding of the internal *and* external markets can be really helpful in ensuring that you're the talent expert in your organization.

 Take a Deeper Dive

Read "Learn How to Handle the Unexpected Events that Trigger Turnover" by Shonna Waters.[1] Also consider Griffeth, Hom, and Gaertner's "A Meta-analysis of Antecedents and Correlates of Employee Turnover"[2] and Holtom et al.'s "How Today's Shocks Predict Tomorrow's Leaving."[3]

Let's return to the story.

··

Jen did some additional reflecting and data gathering to figure out whether a percentage point increase in turnover is something to pay attention to. Her company is in the manufacturing sector, but there are many different types of work and workers required to build the product and get it to market. The managers she's dealing with are in the research and development (R&D) organization. Jen isn't exactly sure what they do over there, but she decided to take a look at the turnover numbers in their area. She learns that their turnover average over the last year is 22 percent. What's more, it looks like it has been getting higher each quarter—not a great trend.

Knowing that their turnover rate is 33 percent more than the company sees on average, Jen realized she may have made a mistake in writing the managers off too quickly. She sends an email and asks to schedule a face-to-face meeting. Jen explains that she wants to work together to better understand the issue. The managers accept the invitation. Jen is left with one week to prepare. That sensation in the pit of her stomach just keeps getting worse.

Jen decides to script out some questions for the meeting. She wants to get a better sense for what might be going on in their organization. She also doesn't have room to look like she hasn't done her homework!

··

Reflection

How would you prepare for this meeting? What questions would you want to ask? What would your agenda look like?

_____

_____

_____

_____

_____

_____

_____

_____

_____

When meeting with your stakeholders, it's important to think about your desired outcomes for the meeting. In this case, it will be important to develop a relationship with them, understand more about the context of their concerns, and develop some credibility as a business partner. You'll also want to understand the impact of this issue on their business, which can help you both assess the priority of the issue and build a business case for action.

You may be noticing that although this book is about analytics, we're spending a lot of time not talking about numbers. The reality is that statistics, data, and other numbers make up a small portion of what's important in effective analytics. To be a good analyst, there are three domains that you need to have a good grasp of.

People. Understanding people means understanding HR and the members of your organization so that you're asking good questions. Understanding fundamentals of psychology, like how to motivate employees and teams, comes in handy here. In HR, we need to understand why people work, what they want from their careers, and why they leave organizations. Understanding people also means knowing how to influence and persuade. Influence and persuasion are necessary to secure buy-in and communicate results in a way that resonates with your various stakeholders.

Business. Analytics will have limited impact if they aren't tied to challenges of importance to business leaders. Analysts need to have a thorough understanding of the business process and where the organization generates its competitive advantage.[4] It's critical to understand the issues business leaders care about and where the business is in greatest need of help.

Data. Understanding data is really about two types of expertise: data expertise and analytics expertise. Data expertise involves working directly with data—data extraction, cleaning, transformation, and management. Analytics expertise involves data analysis, data visualization, and validation.

Although data fluency and statistics, particularly more advanced statistics, are newer skills for many HR professionals, in this book you'll see that much of what is needed are things you're already good at—consulting, business acumen, and a deep understanding of the people and people processes in your organization. In Appendix A you can find a more in-depth description of how HR analytics fit into the SHRM competency model.

....

Jen walks into the meeting and the two managers are there, but they aren't alone. Mark, the director of R&D, is there too, and so is another manager Jen doesn't recognize. They are all sitting on one side of the table, so she sits down across from them. She almost expects someone to pull out a rotten tomato and take aim.

Jen isn't afraid to admit when she's wrong—she acknowledges that she'd been too quick to close the issue. She shares that she learned that turnover in their organization is twice as high as the company-wide average. Jen continues, "I recognize that you're in the best position to know what might be causing this. You can help me understand the impact on the business." She asks them to help educate her.

Jen gets through her introduction, pauses, and looks around the room. Their faces look a little bit softer than when she walked in, so Jen decides it's safe to ask a question. "So tell me more about your concerns."

The four of them glance at each other before the director, Elise, responds.

"We've got an important job to do in our area. It's a competitive market out there and it's our job to not only solve any problems with the product's current functionality, but also to figure out what the next version should look like. Not just the next iteration, but what it needs to look like five years out so that our competitors don't get ahead of us. It can be a high-pressure job. We're kind of asking people to predict—and then create—the future."

One of the managers jumps in. "It can be a lot of pressure, but that's what we all came here to do. Lately though, some of our best people have been leaving. It really isn't just how many are leaving—it's who is leaving."

Another manager adds, "Last week Lin resigned. She was only one person but she was probably responsible for half of the innovations that have come out of our group in the last eighteen months. I don't know how we're going to replace her."

Jen decides to jump in. "Do you have a sense of why she left?"

"She said she had a better opportunity. But who knows? Obviously something motivated her to seek out a better opportunity in the first place."

Jen doesn't conduct the exit interviews, so she doesn't know why Lin or the others left. She asks, "What about the others who left? Have they shared why they were leaving?"

"It's been pretty vague, but we think they're being wooed away by companies that can pay more. These skills are marketable and there's not much we can do other than start paying them more."

After chatting for a while, Jen leaves a bit unsatisfied. It's clear what they think the solution is—more pay. She knows that the company generally takes a lead approach to its compensation strategy for these roles because it is such a competitive market. It's unclear what evidence they're basing that on. It's also unclear whether pay is the only explanation.

···

Reflection

What are the most important pieces of information you garnered from this meeting? What did you learn about their context and impact?

_____

_____

_____

_____

_____

Let's review what Jen learned from the meeting. It's clear that the managers have a hypothesis: people are leaving because of pay; if the company pays more, turnover will decrease. What evidence does Jen have to support that hypothesis? Are there any competing hypotheses that she could test? This is where data and analytics can really help. In the past, HR had to manage by hunch. Today we have more data at our disposal to bring more science and evidence into our decision-making.

Jen also learned a few things about the context of the department:

- It may be a stressful environment, but the managers believe that's part of the draw of the department, not a reason to leave.
- The mission of the department requires innovation.
- The managers believe that a few high performers, including a recent departure, are responsible for the bulk of the organization's performance.
- It sounds like there's currently more speculation than data backing up their current hypothesis.

In the next couple of chapters, we will assess the data the organization currently has available to test the managers' hypothesis and to address the broader question of why people are leaving. We will also review where the holes are and how we might pursue filling in the gaps. Finally, we'll talk about how to go back to the stakeholders with some assessments about what the issues might be and where to go next.

 From the SHRM Research Lab

As I mentioned in Chapter 1, people can be resistant to relying on data or algorithms to make decisions. Analytic evidence can be perceived as a threat, given its potential to develop conclusions contradictory to one's personal judgment. Developing analytic skills in HR professionals is critical to building the foundation for a broader evidence-based approach.

An evidence-based approach means using established methods to identify what works, in what way, and for whom.[5] A 2012 survey of 950 American HR practitioners found large discrepancies between what practitioners think is effective and what current research shows to be effective.[6]

The Center for Evidence-Based Management (CEBMa) describes the four sources of evidence that should be taken into account:[7]

- **Scientific literature:** findings from empirical studies published in academic journals

- **Organizational context:** data, facts, and figures gathered from the organization
- **Practitioner experience and expertise:** professional experience and judgment of practitioners
- **Stakeholders:** values and concerns of people affected by the decisions

Analytic skills are required to appraise and incorporate evidence from all of these sources. See a visualization of this in Figure 2.1.

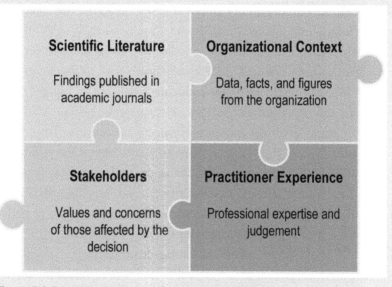

Figure 2.1. Sources of evidence for decision-making

 Key Takeaways

- Consideration of the data at your disposal—both from within and outside of your organization—is essential to answering HR questions.
- HR analytics goes beyond number crunching. Knowledge of people, business, and data are all essential components of an effective HR analyst.

- Questioning your stakeholders to better understand their hypotheses and the context of the given problem will provide you with some of the information necessary to frame your thinking about the issue.

Management Concepts Identifies the Need for On-the-Job Support for Training

Management Concepts is a third-party training company founded in 1973. In 2014, Management Concepts began the process of automating its collection of end-of-course evaluations and ninety-day follow-up evaluations using Metrics That Matter. As of 2016, however, Management Concepts was still using these data only for tactical purposes: reviewing student satisfaction with facilities, customer service, and instructors after each course delivery to improve operations and the student experience. Management Concepts wanted to learn more about the impact the training was having. To get more from the data, they took an aggregate-level look at forty thousand end-of-course evaluations and follow-up evaluations to determine if the training affected business impact and learning effectiveness, and whether training evaluations predicted improvements in performance at ninety days post-training.

Through these analyses, Management Concepts was able to identify a major area that was weak: on-the-job support for training.

Evaluation items related to this area included the following:

- My supervisor and I set expectations for this learning prior to attending this training.
- After training, my supervisor and I will discuss how I will use the learning on my job.
- I will be provided adequate resources (time, money, equipment) to successfully apply this training on my job.

Average scores for these items were up to one full point lower than ratings of other items. As a third-party provider, Management Concepts could not directly influence the on-the-job support participants experienced. They knew, however, that on-the-job support was a critical factor in the effectiveness of the training they were providing. They decided to share the data with the organizations that sent a large number of participants to training. The data were used to get the organizations to think more about how to prepare for training and make the training stick to ensure the companies maximized their return on investment (ROI).

Management Concepts created summaries of the results of the training evaluations for clients. These one-page reports highlighted the degree to which participants felt that the training improved their performance at ninety days post-training, and their general experience in training. They highlighted the results for on-the-job support for clients as a "missed opportunity" and recommended specific steps for them to take to prepare their employees for training as well as improve on-the-job application. This analytics application demonstrates how Management Concepts used data that were already being collected in a new way to create actionable recommendations for their clients.

Endnotes

1. Shonna Waters, "Learn How to Handle the Unexpected Events that Trigger Turnover," *HR Magazine*, October 2017, https://www.shrm.org/hr-today/news/hr-magazine/1017/Pages/learn-how-to-handle-the-unexpected-events-that-trigger-turnover.aspx.

2. Rodger W. Griffeth, Peter W. Hom, and Stefan Gaertner, "A Meta-analysis of Antecedents and Correlates of Employee Turnover: Update, Moderator Tests, and Research Implications for the Next Millennium," *Journal of Management* 26, no. 3 (2000): 463–88.

3. Brooks Holtom et al., "How Today's Shocks Predict Tomorrow's Leaving," *Journal of Business and Psychology* 32, no. 1 (2017): 59–71.

4. Alec Levenson, *Strategic Analytics: Advancing Strategy Execution and Organizational Effectiveness* (Oakland: Berrett-Koehler Publishers, 2015).

5.   Future Work Centre, *"Think Like a Scientist!": Finding Out What Works, in What Way and for Whom*, white paper (Future Work Centre, July 2016), http://www.futureworkcentre.com/wp-content/uploads/2016/09/Think-like-a-scientist-white-paper.pdf.
6.   Sara L. Rynes, "The Research-Practice Gap in I/O Psychology and Related Fields: Challenges and Potential Solutions," in *The Oxford Handbook of Organizational Psychology*, vol. 1, ed. Steve W. J. Kozlowski (Oxford: Oxford University Press, 2012), 409–52.
7.   Eric Barends, Denise Rousseau, and Rob Briner, *Evidence-Based Management: The Basic Principles, white paper* (Amsterdam: Center for Evidence-Based Management, 2014), https://www.cebma.org/wp-content/uploads/Evidence-Based-Practice-The-Basic-Principles.pdf.

3

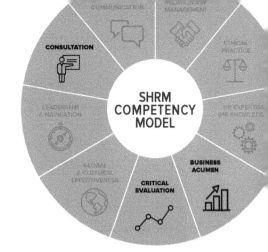

Establish
an Effective
Team

Chapter Snapshot

Questions we will answer:

- How do I build an effective team to tackle the problem I'm facing?
- How do I mobilize my team to execute the work that's needed?
- What are the things my team must agree on to move forward with an analytics project?

....

After meeting with the R&D managers, Jen has a little more context on what the organization does. She learned that innovation is critical. She also learned that the managers feel like a few high performers drive a lot of that innovation. Those high performers include some of the people who have left. Overall, most of what they have to go on for what's driving turnover is speculative. Jen goes back to her office and decides she wants to get a few more brains on this; she wants to talk through it with some colleagues. She needs to figure out if pay is the real issue here. Is there evidence to support that claim? Jen asks her managers across the relevant functions to come to the table. She brings in the HR business partner (HRBP) who serves the R&D organization, the talent acquisition manager, the compensation and benefits manager, and the organizational effectiveness specialist.

....

Many organizations are siloed, even within HR. Often, HR is specialized in areas like recruiting, compensation, employee relations, and so forth. Analytics, especially more advanced analytics, requires a systems perspective. In other words, data must be aligned across the HR function to address broader business challenges. This means problem-solving and analysis can't happen in a vacuum. It's important to connect with others who have valuable insights to add.

Thinking about Jen's situation, why did she choose the people she did? What skills and perspectives do they bring to the table? Well, let's think about it:

- **The R&D HRBP** has insight into the norms and processes of the team that's experiencing the problem.
- **The talent acquisition manager** knows the job market and the company's applicants; he also might know why candidates decline offers.
- **The compensation and benefits manager** has compensation data and has the background to know how to adjust the compensation strategy should she need to. She should also be in the loop because she oversees what the managers want to address.
- **The organizational effectiveness specialist** has unique insight into how employees feel about the organization and their jobs.

 Take a Deeper Dive

There are a lot of things to consider when building your team. Learn more about how to form a high-performing team by reading "Developing and Sustaining High-Performance Work Teams," an online toolkit by the Society for Human Resource Management (SHRM).[1]

After bringing the team up to speed on the situation, Jen asks for their thoughts. The compensation and benefits manager clearly feels on the defensive. She starts explaining the compensation philosophy and where these positions fall relative to the market. The talent acquisition manager starts explaining his recruiting strategy, assuring Jen that the next candidates will be just as strong as the employees they've lost. Jen calls for a time-out. No one should feel defensive. This is an opportunity to help the organization take a deep dive and solve a problem. It's like they're trying to solve a mystery, but first they need more clues. How can they learn more about what might be going on?

The team seems nervous. Jen senses that they might be lacking confidence. She shares with them that data isn't her favorite part of the job, but in reality they work with data all the time. They talk to managers and employees every day. What they learn in those conversations is data too—it's just qualitative. They also keep track of all sorts of metrics throughout the organization. Everything from how many employees they have and where, to how many promotions they can offer this year. They all know the people. Partnering with the R&D organization is going to help them understand the business even better than they already do.

Reflection

How might the team members be feeling? What might be causing their reactions and resistance to Jen's pitch?

_____

_____

_____

_____

_____

It's likely Jen's team is feeling threatened. For some, like the compensation manager, this project may challenge their own work. Could the team's findings hurt her reputation? For others, the idea of collecting data, analyzing it, and testing hypotheses might seem too daunting. Any chance you can empathize?

When you build a team with others, be clear from the beginning that solving a problem isn't a threat to anyone. Putting existing practices under the microscope doesn't have to mean that someone's done a bad job. It's always worthwhile to see where and how you can do better. Furthermore, engaging in this kind of work could actually make your team look better. You're being proactive. Framing your project this way can elicit buy-in. Let your colleagues know what's in it for them. Also, to preempt hard feelings or resistance, it's good practice to involve the individuals who oversee areas relevant to your analyses (like Jen did with the compensation manager). If you start with the right approach, you should be able to ease any defensive feelings.

But what about the intimidation factor? When we hear the term "data" we tend to think about *quantitative* data—numbers. This is the kind of information that yields metrics such as turnover percentages, absenteeism rates, engagement ratings, and time to hire. Like Jen told her team, we all work with *qualitative* data every day. Each time we interact with someone to get information, we're collecting it. Qualitative data are human observations. It's information that can't be easily measured but is valuable nonetheless. Qualitative data may come to us in many forms, such as exit interview responses, reasons for declining a job offer, or performance goals.

Reflection

What are some examples of quantitative data that you use regularly at work? What about qualitative data? Which do you use more regularly?

_____

_____

_____

_____

_____

_____

_____

_____

Jen is able to get her team on board by easing them into data. It helps that some of her team members, like the compensation manager, are used to working with numbers. To really start getting their hands dirty, they need to make sure they're all on the same page with the data and metrics they currently use. Jen assigns each person to a stakeholder from her previous meeting. She tasks them with figuring out how that person's department defines each metric they use. When looking at turnover, are they all using the same figures? If they don't have agreement here, it's going to be tough to report findings to all of the stakeholders.

Reflection

Do the stakeholders in your organization agree on the definitions of basic metrics? Poll a few members of your organization. Ask them to define each of the following metrics. How do their answers match up? (As an added bonus, you're currently collecting qualitative data!)

- Head count
- Hires
- Turnover
- Promotion
- Diversity

_____

_____

_____

_____

_____

_____

_____

_____

_____

_____

How did your coworkers do? If you found any disagreement, you've noticed that even the building blocks of HR analytics aren't so cut-and-dried. Here are just some of the factors that might have complicated your data collection:

- **Head count:** Who counts as an employee?
- **Hires:** When does the hire actually occur? Is it the offer date, or the acceptance date? Who counts as an applicant versus a candidate?
- **Turnover:** What is the denominator we use? Is it the beginning head count or the average head count?
- **Promotion:** What is the denominator we use? Is it the average head count, all employees, or the employees eligible for promotion?
- **Diversity:** How do you report race and ethnicity?

Being explicit in how you define each of your metrics will set you up for an easier analytic path. In the next chapter we'll begin taking stock of the data we have so we can start getting some answers.

 From the SHRM Research Lab

When building a team to carry out a new endeavor, as with Jen's situation above, it's essential to foster a climate of psychological safety among the team. Psychological safety describes the extent to which members find the team interpersonally nonthreatening. Conditions are perceived as unsafe when roles and tasks are ambiguous, unpredictable, or threatening.[2] When team members feel psychologically safe, they are more likely to share knowledge and raise suggestions for improvements.[3]

To best mobilize your team on a new analytics project, particularly if HR analytics is a new endeavor for anyone on the team, take some steps to build psychological safety. Establish trust by expressing concern for others' welfare.[4] Demonstrate humility. Acknowledge your own fallibility, show tolerance of failure, and solicit feedback to lay the groundwork for psychological safety.[5]

Key Takeaways

- HR analytics can't be siloed. Think about the people who can bring some needed insights or skills and seek their partnership.
- No matter your current role, you're surrounded by data every day. Thinking through the ways you regularly interact with data will help you gain the confidence you need.
- Data and metrics won't lead to actionable recommendations unless everyone is on the same page. Make sure everyone shares a common definition of each piece of the puzzle.

Veterinary Holistic Care Reduces Wait Times with Analytics

Veterinary Holistic Care (VHC) is a privately owned, non-twenty-four-hour veterinary clinic providing medical services by appointment only. Despite offering appointment slots longer than the industry average, the clinic was consistently running behind schedule, resulting in clients being seen by the doctor later than their scheduled appointment time. This was contradictory to the vision of the practice, which was focused on providing quality, personalized care, because the doctors and staff often felt rushed and harried when they were running late. It also resulted in increased payroll costs, as staff were frequently held late to complete the final appointments and closing duties.

To establish the scope of the problem, VHC first tracked the number of appointments that were seen late in each day—"late" here defined as more than five minutes past the scheduled appointment time. They tracked this information over the course of a three-month period, and established an average baseline of on-time appointments of roughly 48 percent. VHC then asked for staff feedback on any potential efficiency roadblocks they were encountering. The practice manager also spent several days on the floor observing the workflow. The feedback and observations indicated that having additional support staff would be beneficial to the overall efficiency of the clinic. Finally, VHC compared the number of scheduled hours with the number of hours worked during the previously tracked quarter. Actual hours worked exceeded the number of scheduled hours by roughly 17 percent. VHC concluded that their current doctor to staff ratio of 1:3 was insufficient for the needs of the clinic.

VHC determined that adding one full-time employee to the staff would result in more on-time appointments, as well as a reduction in the number of hours employees were working beyond their scheduled hours. The savings in staff overtime was enough to significantly offset the cost of the new hire. After the training period for the new hire was completed, they tracked the number of appointments that were being seen late over the course of a new three-month period, as well as the number of hours worked beyond employees' regularly scheduled hours. On-time appointments jumped dramatically from 48 percent to roughly 86 percent—a 38 percentage point increase. Additionally, there were only three instances where staff were held more than fifteen minutes past the end of their shift. With the new 1:4 doctor-to-staff ratio, VHC was able to see an average of 1.4 additional appointments per day.

Endnotes

1. Society for Human Resource Management, "Developing and Sustaining High-Performance Work Teams," toolkit, July 23, 2015, https://www.shrm.org/resourcesandtools/tools-and-samples/toolkits/pages/developingandsustaininghigh-performanceworkteams.aspx.
2. Amy C. Edmondson, "Psychological Safety and Learning Behavior in Work Teams," *Administrative Science Quarterly* 44, no. 2 (1999): 350–83.
3. Jian Liang, Crystal I. C. Farh, and Jing-Lih Farh, "Psychological Antecedents of Promotive and Prohibitive Voice: A Two-Wave Examination," *Academy of Management Journal* 55, no. 1 (2012): 71–92.
4. Johannes M. Pennings and Jaana Woiceshyn, "A Typology of Organizational Control and Its Metaphors," *Research in the Sociology of Organizations* 5, no. 73 (1987): 73–104.
5. Amy C. Edmondson, "Managing the Risk of Learning: Psychological Safety in Work Teams," in *International Handbook of Organizational Teamwork and Cooperative Working*, ed. Michael West, Dean Tjosvold, and Ken Smith (Chichester, Eng.: John Wiley and Sons, 2003), 255–76; and Jia Hu et al., "Leader Humility and Team Creativity: The Role of Team Information Sharing, Psychological Safety, and Power Distance," *Journal of Applied Psychology* 103, no. 3 (2018): 313–23, http://dx.doi.org/10.1037/apl0000277.

4

Form Your Hypothesis

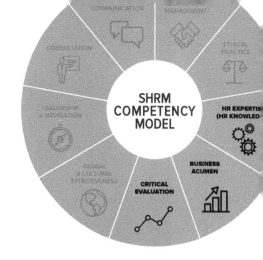

SHRM COMPETENCY MODEL

Chapter Snapshot

Questions we will answer:

- What is a hypothesis?
- What kind of data will I work with when testing a hypothesis?
- Where can I find the data I need to test my hypothesis?

....

Now that Jen's team is on board, they just need to dive deeper into the data. They start by talking about what they each already know well.

The HRBP mentions that they routinely send out exit surveys and that employees have the option to do an exit interview. She points out that they also have performance ratings. The organizational effectiveness specialist mentions the engagement survey. It's only administered annually, but there may be something the team can learn from it. The talent acquisition manager mentions that his team enters some data into the system during the recruiting and hiring process. For example, they use rationale codes to keep track of why candidates turn down a job offer. Salary is one of the rationales included in the codes.

....

Reflection

Aside from what Jen's teammates have mentioned so far, what else might they look into? Where might they uncover more data to get to the bottom of R&D's turnover issue?

_____

_____

_____

_____

_____

Before worrying too much about the data, start with a hypothesis. A *hypothesis* is a prediction about variables of interest. *Variables* are simply anything that can be measured or counted. In HR, we usually work with variables like employee engagement, turnover, salary, and job satisfaction. Starting any analytics project with a hypothesis will help you determine the kind of data you need. A simple way of structuring a hypothesis is as an *if / then* statement. The R&D managers have a hypothesis about turnover in their department: low pay is explaining the turnover problem. Put another way, they hypothesize that *if* R&D employees are paid more, *then* they will be less likely to leave the organization.

It's important to look at multiple hypotheses. If your initial hypothesis isn't supported, you'll have little direction for moving forward. If Jen only considers the managers' hypothesis, what happens if she finds out pay doesn't explain the turnover problem? She can't propose alternative solutions without investigating alternative hypotheses.

Think about the other sources of data Jen's team mentioned. Look at your responses to the reflection above. You've got the components of alternative hypotheses there. Some possible alternative hypotheses are that employees are leaving because

- they aren't engaged in their work,
- they don't have good relationships with their coworkers, or
- they don't get along with their supervisors.

Thinking through viable alternative hypotheses will help you get a sense of where to find data in your organization.

When trying to uncover data, don't be afraid to get creative. Sure, looking at turnover percentages and exit interview responses are viable options. But think outside of the box to get a fuller sense of the situation. Sometimes the things you'd least expect actually have a big impact on the bottom line. For example, a large financial firm did some digging into the drivers of high performance. They found that GPAs, quality of references, and attendance at a top universities didn't matter. Things like lack of misspellings in résumés and related sales experience *did* matter in predicting top performance.[1]

Start by brainstorming. Think about the information that may be available. Is there a way it might be relevant? What sources are available to you? Do you use an applicant tracking system (ATS)? What information does it collect? Is there customer-driven data somewhere? What kind of content is available via performance reviews? What information do you have about the context (department, supervisor, direct reports, etc.)? Be as inclusive as you can.

Jen's team is off to a great start! Jen gives assignments to each of them to dig around and see what they have. She also asks the compensation and benefits manager to put something together to show their salary ranges relative to the market. She poses a question to the group: "How can we learn more? What would be more compelling to R&D managers?"

The compensation and benefits manager offers a suggestion. If the team can give her a list of everyone who's left the organization in the last few years, she can look up their pay history. She can see not just where they were in the salary range, but also what other kinds of rewards they'd gotten during their tenure.

Let's think about the data Jen's team is pooling. They've got a number of metrics at their disposal. Her team has covered areas from recruitment through departure. Now let's dig a little deeper. Once you've started identifying sources of information, it's time to consider what kind of information you're getting.

In data analytics, there are four different types of variables you can work with: nominal, ordinal, interval, and ratio. Figure 4.1 summarizes these types of variables. *Nominal* variables are usually qualitative. You can think of nominal data as categorical—each variable is broken up into different categories. These variables are qualitatively, not quantitatively, different. You can't have more or less of something in nominal terms. An example of a nominal variable in HR would be department. To look at how something differs across departments, you'd have to categorize employees by this variable: R&D, HR, finance, and so on. One department isn't more or less than another; they're just different.

Ordinal variables are rank-ordered. For example, if employees were ranked from best to worst in terms of sales performance, you'd be working with an ordinal variable. The other two types of variables have clearer counting systems.

Interval variables indicate whether a data point is higher or lower than another as well as by how much. The spacing between each unit on an

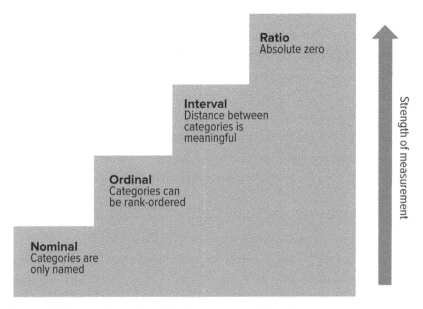

Figure 4.1. Types of variables. Each category builds on the previous one

interval scale is even and meaningful. Interval variables aren't common in HR, but an example of one would be temperature in degrees Fahrenheit. You know that a temperature of 90°F is higher than a temperature of 70°F. More specifically, you know it's exactly 20°F higher. The other defining characteristic of interval variables is an arbitrary zero point. Sticking with the temperature example, 0°F doesn't mean there's no temperature—in fact, the temperature can still get lower.

Ratio variables have all of the properties of interval variables, but they also have an absolute zero point. This means that a value of zero indicates a total absence of something. In HR, we may look at employee absences as a variable. This would be a ratio variable because zero absences means a complete lack of absences at work.

There is another meaningful way to distinguish the types of information you're using. The metrics you work with can be classified as either lagging or leading indicators (see Figure 4.2).

Lagging indicators are metrics describing what happened in the past. "Lagging" refers to the time lapse between an action and a specific outcome. These can cover workforce-related expenditures, cost per hire, position fill rates, and turnover.

Leading indicators are metrics that provide early indications of your progress toward an objective. Employee engagement scores, selection test and training scores, employee retention rates, intention to leave, and position vacancy days are all examples of leading indicators.

Lagging and leading indicators work together, allowing you to make a more comprehensive evaluation. Think about recruiting as an example of this. Your organization likely collects a lot of information on sourcing:

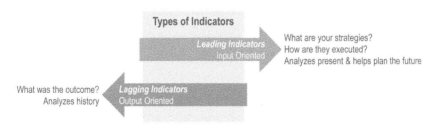

Figure 4.2. Lagging vs. leading indicators

amount of traffic on career sites, social media following, number of new candidates entering the application system, and so on. These leading indicators will tell you what you're doing now and give you a sense of how well it's working. But it isn't until you combine that information with lagging indicators, like the number of offers accepted, that you get a full sense of your recruitment approach and its effectiveness.

> **Reflection**
>
> Think about the data Jen's team is compiling. See Table 4.1 for a summary.
>
> Which of these are lagging indicators? Which are leading? How might you use each of them to understand turnover in R&D?
>
> _____
>
> _____
>
> _____
>
> _____
>
> _____

Did you struggle at all with the reflection above? If you did, it's likely because many of the variables could be leading _or_ lagging indicators depending on the outcome of interest. For example, performance review scores would be a lagging indicator if Jen were examining the effectiveness of a training program. But Jen's team is interested in turnover, so performance ratings would be a leading indicator. Performance ratings could possibly be used to gain early insight into turnover in R&D.

....

All of these data sources make Jen think that looking at turnover alone isn't enough. The team can't just look at the employees who left. They'd be neglecting a huge pool of information by ignoring the current employees. Moreover, the team can't link anonymous engagement survey data with specific separations. The organizational effectiveness specialist mentions that there are turnover-intent questions on the engagement survey. A section of the survey asks

Table 4.1. Data summary

Data collector	Data sets
Organizational Effectiveness Specialist	Employee engagement survey scores
HRBP	Performance review scores
	Exit interviews
Compensation and Benefits Manager	Industry-wide salary ranges
	Range penetration of separated employees
	Salary history of separated employees
Talent Acquisition Manager	Recruiting data (e.g., offer decline rationale codes)

employees about their likelihood of leaving in the near future. Jen notes that turnover-intent data would be a great leading indicator of turnover in R&D.

Jen congratulates the team on contributing such good ideas. She shares that she has been reading a lot about the power of storytelling and thinks being able to talk about specific cases of departure will be a great way to capture the managers' attention. Everyone agrees to regroup once they've had a chance to do some homework.

As Jen moves along in the data collection process, it's time to think about how her team moves forward. In applying these practices at your own organization, this will require an honest assessment of your team. Your approach to analytics will vary depending on the kind of data you have and the level of your team's analytics expertise.

Bersin by Deloitte developed a widely used HR analytics maturity model. It features four levels, each representing increasing complexity in the type of analytics used.[2]

Levels 1 and 2 are different flavors of HR reporting. Organizations at Level 1, *operational reporting*, use data and metrics to understand what happened in the past (and maybe why). At Level 1, your function might be focused on understanding the data available and getting agreement on what they mean. The reflection activity from Chapter 3 where we defined some common metrics had us working at Level 1. At Level 2, *advanced reporting*, reporting becomes more proactive or routine. Level 2 reporting

People Analytics Maturity Model

Source: Bersin, Deloitte Consulting LLP, 2018.

Figure 4.3. HR analytics maturity model

may even be automated and presented in dashboards. At this level you might begin looking at relationships among variables.

HR functions operating at Level 3, *strategic analytics*, may be developing causal models. In other words, they're trying to explain why something is happening—for example, by assessing drivers of turnover or engagement. Level 3 might look at how those relationships affect outcomes, either positively or negatively. Those at Level 4, *predictive analytics*, are making predictions and using those predictions to plan for the future. An example might be using turnover, promotion, and market data to model scenarios that help with workforce planning.

Reflection

Think about Jen's turnover situation in R&D. Essentially, she wants to know if pay is causing the spike in turnover. If it isn't, what is? Now think about the HR analytics maturity model. Let's work through it. If Jen were addressing this question from each level of the model, what data would she need? What might she investigate? What results might she report?

- Level 1: Operational reporting

  _____

  _____

  _____

  _____

  _____

- Level 2: Advanced reporting

  _____

  _____

  _____

  _____

  _____

- Level 3: Strategic analytics

  _____

  _____

  _____

- Level 4: Predictive analytics

  _____

  _____

  _____

  _____

  _____

What level of maturity would you say your department is currently at? If you're still focused more on reporting than analytics—meaning you're at Levels 1 or 2—don't fret. Bersin by Deloitte found that 56 percent of organizations are operating at Level 1, and 30 percent are at Level 2. Don't worry if you aren't as far along in the model as you'd like to be. And definitely don't push to advance too quickly. Rather than aiming for a big bang initially, stay focused and generate some quick wins. Start with the data you have. Look for critical business problems that offer an opportunity for impact. Depending on the business problem, advancing beyond Level 2 may not be necessary. For example, if your company is seeing low engagement and wants to get to the bottom of it, it might be enough to describe the state of the workforce as it is. What are you seeing in climate surveys, exit interviews, and other sources? Taking this kind of approach will help you create a virtuous cycle where results lead to greater investment. That increased investment enables more results, in turn generating even more investment.

It's also worth noting that these levels don't work in isolation. Often, your data can be applied to multiple levels of analysis. Sometimes you're even operating at multiple levels at once. After all, these levels build on one another. You couldn't conduct analyses at Level 4 without first understanding your data and knowing what they mean. In the next chapter, we'll start talking about the ways you might address an HR issue at Levels 1 and 2. Then in Chapter 6 we'll get into more advanced techniques that are likely to push you into Levels 3 and 4.

 Take a Deeper Dive

Read "How to Set Up Your Workforce Analytics Function."[3]

 From the SHRM Research Lab

If you picked up this book because you've been feeling the pressure to get acquainted with HR analytics, then it's possible you've heard some talk about big data. The term "big data" describes data sets that are expansive in terms of the three V's:[4]

- **Volume:** Big data sets may contain upward of one quadrillion bytes of data.
- **Velocity:** Devices like radio-frequency identification (RFID) chips and sensors allow data to be handled practically in real time.
- **Variety:** Big data come from a variety of sources and in all types of formats (numbers, text, audio, etc.).

You might be wondering how this affects you and your colleagues. Does HR have big data? The answer depends on the size of the organization, the nature of the business, and the data and questions at hand. If you are using multiple years of HR data from hundreds of thousands of employees to predict outcomes in hundreds of thousands or millions of cases, the amount of data may be part of the problem. In most HR organizations, this is not a problem.

Capelli argues that HR's problem isn't because of the amount of data we have to deal with, but rather its storage.[5] HR data often reside in different databases that usually aren't readily compatible. This means that database managers and tools to make progress on the basics are likely a better starting point than advanced analyses.

Data mining is a common way of handling big data. It's used to analyze big data and overcome some of the limitations of human information processing and traditional analytic techniques. This approach applies machine learning algorithms to find patterns of relationships between elements in large, messy data sets.[6] The objective of data mining is to use the detected patterns to predict future outcomes and make better decisions.

Take a Deeper Dive

Read "How Midsized Businesses Can Take Advantage of Big Data: Seven Practical Tips for Getting Started with Data Visualization," a white paper by SAS.[7]

Key Takeaways

- Hypotheses build the foundation for data analytics. Develop alternative hypotheses to explain the issue at hand. These hypotheses will guide your data collection.
- When identifying potential sources of data, be as inclusive as possible. There may be explanations that don't match your hypothesis; you'll never uncover those if you ignore the

data at your disposal. Leverage different types of variables and both leading and lagging indicators to give you a more comprehensive sense of your organization.

- Regardless of the maturity of your analytics function, you can leverage what you have available to tackle a business problem. Demonstrating the utility of HR analytics is likely to advance support for deeper analyses in the future.

Microstrategy Helps Employees Drive Healthy Habits

Like many companies today, MicroStrategy, an enterprise analytics and mobility software company headquartered in northern Virginia, was looking for new ways to support and engage its employees in healthy habits with the goal of improving productivity and general well-being. One area that had considerable interest and support from employees was in employee fitness. After evaluating options for how to best support employee fitness goals, MicroStrategy decided to partner with Fitbit to provide Fitbit devices for employees globally at reduced rates. Using Microstrategy's own analytics software, the company created a set of dashboards to gamify the employee fitness program and further incentivize employees.

Through the Fitbit partnership, all MicroStrategy employees have the option to purchase a Fitbit at a very low price. The Fitbit collects data on physical activity, including exercise time, steps, and number of stairs climbed, that serve as key indicators for engagement in any variety of wellness activities. Through an application programming interface (API; code that allows two software programs to communicate) available from Fitbit, MicroStrategy could feed employee Fitbit data into its enterprise analytics platform to create reports on employee activity, tailored for specific contests that emphasize different fitness goals. During one quarter, employees were challenged to spend at least twenty minutes per day engaged in exercise that increased heart rate and to walk at least 7,500 steps. The data collected from Fitbit was fed into a report that provided daily feedback and a scoreboard of who was most active across the company (Figure 4.4).

Using MicroStrategy's data and dashboard technology allows the company to use the fundamentals of behavioral psychology to shape and drive its employee fitness program. Quarter over quarter, employee participation in the program grows. The employee fitness dashboard (Figure 4.5) is available company-wide and shows how many employees participate in the program and key metrics of those participating, such as average active minutes, number of steps, and floors climbed on a daily basis. Further, employees can look at performance from a discipline and team level, allowing the company to create new games that nudge wellness behavior in different ways.

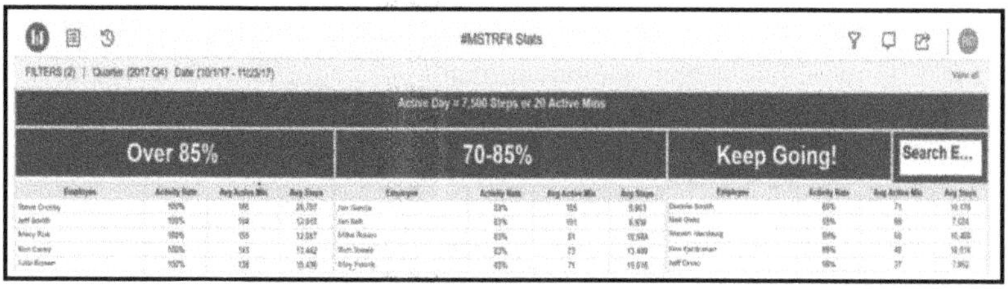

Figure 4.4. MicroStrategy Employee Fitness Report

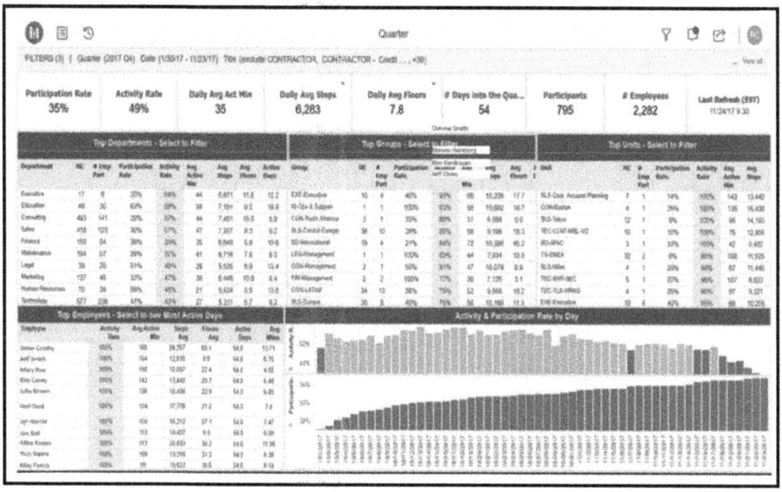

Figure 4.5. MicroStrategy Employee Fitness Dashboard

Endnotes

1. Josh Bersin, "The Datafication of HR," *Deloitte Review*, no. 14 (January 17, 2014), https://www2.deloitte.com/insights/us/en/deloitte-review/issue-14/dr14-datafication-of-hr.html.

2. Bersin, "Datafication of HR."

4. "How to Set Up Your Workforce Analytics Function," https://www.visier.com/lp/set-up-workforce-analytics-function/.

5. Doug Laney, "3D Data Management: Controlling Data Volume, Velocity, and Variety," in *Application Delivery Strategies* (META Group, 2001), https://blogs.gartner.com/doug-laney/files/2012/01/ad949-3D-Data-Management-Controlling-Data-Volume-Velocity-and-Variety.pdf.

6. Peter Capelli, "There's No Such Thing as Big Data in HR," *Harvard Business Review*, July 7, 2017, http://www.hbr.org/2017/06/theres-no-such-thing-as-big-data-in-hr.

7. Robert Nisbet, John Elder, and Gary Miner, *Handbook of Statistical Analysis and Data Mining Applications* (Cambridge, MA: Academic Press, 2009).

8. SAS, *How Midsized Businesses Can Take Advantage of Big Data: Seven Practical Tips for Getting Started with Data Visualization*, white paper (SAS, 2017), https://www.sas.com/content/dam/SAS/en_us/doc/whitepaper1/midmarket-can-take-advantage-of-big-data-107440.pdf.

5

Run Basic
Analyses

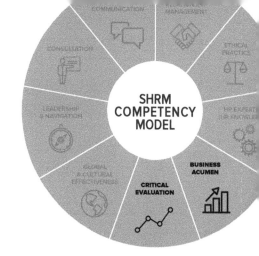

SHRM
COMPETENCY
MODEL

Chapter Snapshot

Questions we will answer:

- How do I identify what data and metrics to look for?
- What are some basic analytics that I can run on my data?
- How can I support a specific hypothesis?

Jen's team does their homework and regroups. When they get together, it becomes clear that the story isn't so simple. Engagement scores aren't great in the R&D organization (see Figure 5.1). Although they're higher than the organizational average for certain dimensions, like meaningfulness of work, they're lower than average for management and supervision, as well as awards and recognition. Employees seem to say that they believe they can be paid more elsewhere. But they also say that they love their work and their colleagues.

Before the team dives deeper into the engagement scores, Jen decides to look at the recruiting data. Talent acquisition asked candidates who declined an offer of employment for their rationale. There isn't a lot of good evidence there either. The rationales are all over the place. What's worse is that the more closely Jen examines the responses, the more confused she gets. She can't identify the top reason candidates weren't accepting offers. As she digs into the data, Jen notices that the codes are wrong. She can't follow the story.

	R&D Average	Company Average	
About my work and my position	**77%**	**80%**	
Being paid competitively with the local market	72%	85%	
Meaningfulness of my work	89%	81%	
Confident I can meet my goals	86%	84%	
Passion and excitement for my work	61%	69%	
About management	**63%**	**69%**	
Awards and recognition by management	57%	68%	
Relationship with management and supervision	56%	70%	
Communication between employees and senior management	71%	67%	
Management expectations are clear	68%	72%	
About the organization	**85%**	**86%**	
Organization's commitment to my professional development	73%	79%	
Overal corporate culture	87%	85%	
Relationships with colleagues	96%	92%	
Overall life and work balance	85%	86%	

Figure 5.1. Engagement scores in R&D compared to the rest of the company

Think about the typical survey questions you see in your job. How often are the responses numbers? It's probably not very often. Questions more commonly ask employees to choose a phrase that best describes their situation. Sometimes responses are open-ended, meaning individuals write in their own responses. When either of these happen, survey data are recoded.

What is recoding? Recoding is simply converting text into a number. This makes the data easier to analyze. In Jen's case, the talent acquisition group coded the reasons why candidates declined employment offers. Table 5.1 shows some of their data. Based on the legend that came with her data, the number 1 should represent that the candidate was not happy with the salary offered. A code of 2 should indicate that the candidate accepted another offer, and so on. But when Jen looked at the data, this wasn't always the case. The rationale for declining an offer wasn't always recoded into the correct number. Jen discovered this error by comparing the actual survey responses with the recoded data. The two sources weren't lining up.

Spotting the abnormality in Jen's data was straightforward. She looked closely at the data and saw that the open-ended response "Dissatisfied with compensation" was coded as a 1 for one candidate and 5 for another. There were other inconsistencies. A code of 2 was assigned to two different responses: "Personal reasons" and "Position is not as described." Some responses weren't directly useful. One response just said "Salary and benefits package." It's unclear what this means. Was the salary too low? Was the benefits package lacking? There's no way of knowing based on the data Jen has.

Jen isn't alone here. Problems in data sets aren't uncommon. In fact, it's pretty rare that you'll find an organizational data set that doesn't require some cleaning. So it's important to visually inspect your data for

Table 5.1. Reasons why candidates declined an employment offer

Candidate	Reason for Rejection	Rationale Code
A	Dissatisfied with compensation	1
B	Dissatisfied with compensation	5
C	Personal reasons	2
D	Accepted another offer	Other
E	Lack of growth opportunity	—
F	Position is not as described	2
G	Decided to stay at current job	Other
H	Salary and benefits package	Other
I	Poor cultural fit	3
J	Accepted another offer	—
K	Distance to work location	Other

any issues before moving on. The main problems you'll want to screen for are missing data and outliers.

Missing data are almost inevitable in analytics. This occurs whenever a data value—a code or number—is absent. Look at the data before you analyze them. Are any values missing? Data points can go missing for several reasons. A common reason for missing data is nonresponse. For instance, when an applicant doesn't provide ethnicity or gender information for your Equal Employment Opportunity Commission (EEOC) reporting, there's no data captured for it. However, missing data can also reflect an error in data entry. In Jen's case, many recruitment codes were missing even though candidates provided responses. This was an error that happened during coding.

Missing data can pose more or less of a problem depending on how random they are. Missing values scattered haphazardly throughout your data set may be inconvenient, but they don't necessarily pose a threat to your analyses. When missing data follow a clearer pattern, there may be a problem. In those cases, you might need to revisit how you collect your data. For example, if you notice that a lot of demographic information is missing in your recruitment data, you might need to rethink how you're asking these questions. Maybe candidates need to have more rationale for including that information or understand how it will be used to feel comfortable sharing it.

For Jen, it was easy to spot the issues with coding. She could detect them just by looking at a few data points. If you have a large data set, this may not be so simple. In those cases, you might want to create a frequency distribution. A frequency distribution is a table that displays how many times each value or category of a variable occurred. Table 5.2 shows a frequency distribution for Jen's recruitment data. Recall from Table 5.1 that she was given data for 11 candidates. As you can see in Table 5.2, only 9 responses are accounted for. This suggests that some data are missing.

An *outlier* is a data point that is substantially different than the other values in the data set. These points do not reflect what's typical of your data. They have such extreme values that they can distort analyses. Let's say you're looking into salaries in a particular department and they range

Table 5.2. Frequency distribution of job offer decline rationales

Rationale Code	Number of Occurrences
1	1
2	2
3	1
4	0
5	1
Other	4

from $40,000 to $75,000, but the vice president (VP) of that department makes $125,000 per year. If you were to include the VP's salary in your data, it would appear that salaries are a lot more varied than they actually are. This is because the VP's salary is an outlier.

As with missing data, outliers can be easy to detect in smaller data sets. With larger data sets, you'll probably want to look at a graphic representation of your data. A histogram is a straightforward tool for this. You can think of a histogram as the graph version of a frequency distribution. Outliers become apparent because they fall far from where the rest of the data are clustered. Again, let's think about our salary example. Figure 5.2 shows two histograms: one without the VP's salary and one with the VP's salary included. It's clear you have an outlier because one point is so far away from the others.

Take a Deeper Dive

Read *The Ultimate Guide to Basic Data Cleaning* by SocialCops.[1]

....

The recruiting data offered little help. The rationale codes were clearly a mess. The staff wasn't using them consistently and most of them were either blank or "other," another big problem. Jen's to-do list is already very long. She needs to handle this issue before it falls off her radar. Since she knows that coding is an essential component of conducting analyses, Jen talks to the talent acquisition

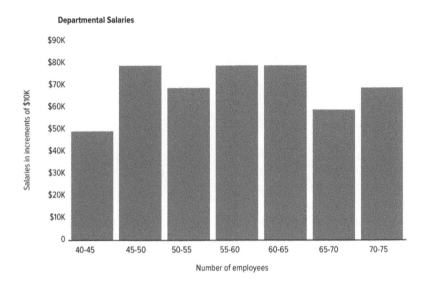

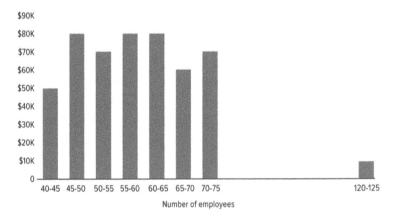

Figure 5.2. Histograms of departmental salaries with (above) and without (below) the VP

manager. They discuss staff training for next year on quality control processes. The two of them build this as an action item and discuss a long-term plan.

Okay, one less thing on Jen's to-do list. But her bigger problem hasn't been solved. She's back to her main issue. What does Jen do now?

She takes a look at the salary data for the R&D department. The salaries for the ten most recent separations are in Table 5.3. How can she start making sense of this information?

Table 5.3. R&D salaries

Employee ID	Salary
6332	93,148
9206	74,859
2823	80,951
5367	73,762
6735	71,686
9422	74,859
5297	74,859
1381	86,646
2443	62,990
7312	60,310

After you've looked at your data for any red flags like outliers or missing data, the next step is usually to take a look at some descriptive statistics. Descriptive statistics are exactly what their name suggests. They are techniques that *describe* your data. Think of them as snapshots of your data. There are two major categories of descriptive statistics: measures of central tendency and variability.

Central tendency describes the center point of your data set. Measures of central tendency tell you where your data are clustering. A measure of central tendency is your best guess for the value, absent other information. There are three specific measures you can use for central tendency: mean, median, and mode. The *mean* is simply the mathematical average. You can calculate it by dividing the sum of all responses by the number of responses. The mean can be heavily affected by any outliers in your data. The *median* is the true midpoint of your data. It's the 50th percentile. If you arrange all of your data points in ascending order, the median is right in the middle. If your data set has any outliers, the median may be a more appropriate measure than the mean. Lastly, the *mode* is the value that occurs most frequently in your data set. When your data are "normally distributed," the mean, median, and the mode will be the same.

If you were to display all of your data points on a graph, a *normal distribution* would resemble a bell curve—a peak in the middle fanning out and down equally on both ends. Imagine splitting the image straight down the middle and folding it in half; the sides would line up with one another. When these two halves don't match, this can indicate an issue with your data—a nonnormal distribution—and your measures of central tendency won't match each other. Figure 5.3 illustrates normal and non-normal distributions.

Take a Deeper Dive

For more on why the normal distribution is so important and how it fits into statistics, read "Normal Distribution" in *HyperStat Online* by David M. Lane.[2]

Reflection

Look again at Table 5.3. It lists the salaries for the ten most recent R&D separations. Describe that data in terms of central tendency. Calculate the mean, median, and mode.

_____

_____

_____

_____

_____

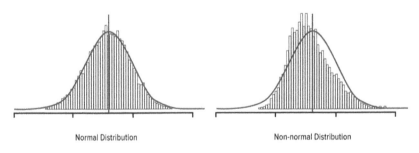

Normal Distribution   Non-normal Distribution

Figure 5.3. Normal vs. nonnormal distributions

Variability can be thought of as the "spread" of your data. Measures of variability tell you how different your data points are from each other. Range and standard deviation are common ways of reporting variability. The *range* is the difference between the largest and smallest values in your data set. Look back to the salary data in Table 5.3. The range of the salaries in R&D is $60,310–$93,148, or $32,838. *Standard deviation* is another way of measuring your data's variability. A low standard deviation means that most of your data are clustered around the mean. The higher your standard deviation, the more dispersed your data are. Figure 5.4 illustrates this.

Calculating measures of central tendency is a skill you're likely to use often. The math for that is fairly straightforward. Calculating variability, on the other hand, involves complex mathematical equations. Statistical software programs or Microsoft Excel can provide you with the standard deviation and many other indicators you may need.

Take a Deeper Dive
Read "Descriptive Statistics in Microsoft Excel" by Maclean, Cipriano, and Zaric.[3]

Measures of central tendency and variability work together to give you a concise summary of your data. When you don't have any outliers, the mean is the most common indicator of central tendency. But on its own, the mean doesn't tell you much. It isn't until you also take the standard

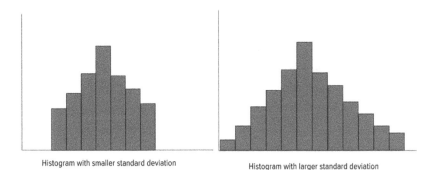

Histogram with smaller standard deviation

Histogram with larger standard deviation

Figure 5.4. Standard deviations and the spread of data

deviation into account that you really have a sense of your data. Let's say you give an employee engagement survey and scores can range from 1 to 5. If you're told the average score on the survey is 3, things look pretty satisfactory. But what if you find out that the standard deviation is 2? This means a lot of employees provided responses that were 2 points away from the mean. In other words, many employees reported engagement scores of 1 or 5. This tells a different story than what just the average would lead you to believe—one that might lead you to take different actions. It might indicate that there are subgroups of employees who are experiencing the organization very differently. What might be causing that? You're likely to miss that by looking at the mean alone.

Percentiles offer another way to understand how a data point fits into the bigger picture. Think again about the salary data presented in Table 5.3. If Jen wanted to understand more about a recent separation's pay, she could look at the percentile score. A *percentile score* tells you what percentage of people fall below an individual on a given metric, so where an individual falls relative to everyone else. If Jen is looking at Employee 1381 relative to the most recent separations, that employee was in the 80th percentile for salary.

Speaking of Jen, let's get back to her analyses.

....

Jen knows she needs more information. She starts digging into the exit data from individuals who left in the last twelve months, and things become even less clear. On paper, the people leaving don't look like top performers. As Figure 5.5 shows, most R&D employees are at least meeting expectations. Jen decides to look at the performance ratings just of the recent separations. They aren't much higher than those of the rest of the department (Table 5.4). There doesn't appear to be a pattern of awards or recognition for them either. In fact, the compensation and benefits manager notes that R&D doesn't seem to be using many of the available tools.

Jen looks at the responses from exit surveys and interviews. She breaks them down and looks at frequencies for each kind of response (see Table 5.5). The data show that people mentioned opportunities for growth and development as often as they mentioned salary. Hmm.

....

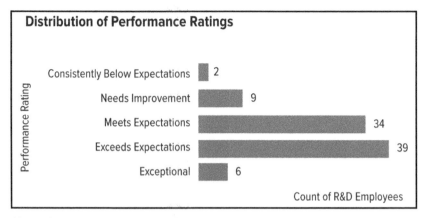

Figure 5.5. Frequency distribution of R&D performance ratings

Table 5.4. Performance ratings of separations versus active employees

Rating	Percent of R&D Separations	Percent of Active R&D Employees
5—Exceptional	8%	7%
4—Exceeds Expectations	44%	43%
3—Meets Expectations	33%	38%
2—Needs Improvement	12%	10%
1—Consistently below Expectations	3%	2%

Jen's data in Table 5.5 are presented as a cross-tabulation, or "cross-tabs" as many call it. This can be a useful tool for getting into more specific elements of your data. Cross-tabs allow you to compare mutually exclusive categories of responses. If you look at each column in Table 5.5, they each represent a different quarter. Each quarter is independent from one another, or mutually exclusive. Some other common examples of mutually exclusive categorical groups are gender, age ranges, and salary.

....

Jen's team has collected some great information. It's getting them closer to discovering what's going on with turnover in R&D. But it doesn't exactly conform to the "pay more" approach the managers were looking for. However, it also doesn't rule that out. Jen is going to need a more cohesive story.

....

Table 5.5. R&D exit data

Reason for Leaving	Q1	Q2	Q3	Q4	2017 Total
Pay is not competitive	1	1	3	3	8
Few developmental opportunities	1	2	3	2	8
Moving or relocation	1	0	0	1	2
Family reasons	0	1	0	1	2
Total	3	4	6	7	20

Reflection

If you were in Jen's shoes, how might you make sense of the situation in R&D? What are some next steps you might take?

_____

_____

_____

_____

_____

_____

_____

_____

_____

The exit interview data suggest that the top two reasons people are leaving are pay and lack of growth and development opportunities. The recruitment data didn't give Jen much insight, but they did highlight that people decline employment in R&D for a variety of reasons. Performance ratings also didn't support the hypothesis that the people leaving were top performers. Managers claim this is true, but if that were the case, wouldn't top performers have higher performance ratings? Or maybe they would have received added incentives while they were in the department? There's no data to support that the separations from R&D were top performers. Jen only has the word of management at this point.

When you're testing a hypothesis of your own, it's likely that you won't quickly arrive at a clear answer. Like Jen, you may find that your data and the claims of your stakeholders don't mesh. This doesn't mean there isn't an answer, and it doesn't necessarily mean the stakeholders are wrong. Usually, this means you've got more work ahead of you! If you find yourself at this juncture, you'll need to consider running more analyses (and possibly collecting more data to do that).

In Jen's case, she needs to be able to show the relationship between pay and turnover. So far, her data has only led to descriptive information. She looked at turnover rates. She found that engagement scores were low. She considered responses from exit interviews, many of them surrounding pay and developmental opportunities. However, nothing is working together. There are multiple pieces, but none of them are talking to each other. In the next chapter, we'll look at the next steps for Jen, and I'll introduce you to some analyses that can be used to explore relationships among your variables.

 From the SHRM Research Lab

In this chapter, we looked at a lot of data from Jen's team. Performance ratings, engagement scores, and other surveys are common sources of HR data. The common denominator here is that all of this data relies on human input. Like I've touched on earlier, humans aren't entirely rational. This can lead to some important considerations for the data you're collecting.

There are a few cognitive biases that commonly distort performance ratings. These inaccuracies may be intentional or due purely to human error in rating. *Central tendency bias* is the inclination to choose a rating somewhere in the middle of a scale, even when a more extreme score (for better or worse) is a better description. Raters often fall into this pattern when more extreme ratings require a written justification.

Leniency error occurs when raters are unusually easy in their ratings, while *severity error* refers to the tendency to be unusually harsh in one's ratings. Sometimes individuals commit these errors because of the language used in a rating scale. Terms like "average" and "outstanding" are relative and may lead a manager to use a personal average rather than an average that other managers may be using.[4]

Halo error is another common cognitive bias in employee ratings. This refers to a "halo" or aura that surrounds all ratings of an individual.[5] If a manager has to rate an employee on several different dimensions, he or she would assign the same rating to that person on every dimension. Sometimes this may be attributable to laziness. But this also can reflect an underlying perception that performance is a singular dimension: people are either good or poor performers.

As with other issues at work, training is a common solution for rating errors. Frame-of-reference training provides managers (or anyone else making ratings) with a context for their evaluations.[6] This kind of training includes information on the multidimensional nature of performance. It also provides raters with an understanding for the anchors included on the rating scale. If a rating of 3 indicates the employee meets expectations, what exactly does that mean? Frame-of-reference training usually involves practice sessions in which raters use the scale to rate hypothetical employees and are given feedback on those ratings.[7]

Many organizations are wrestling with the practical realities of performance ratings. They are time-consuming and, because of biases like the ones above, all that work can still result in suboptimal information. Despite their limitations, performance ratings tend to relate to other outcomes of interest and often inform other organizational decisions such as pay, development, and succession planning. It's important to be aware of the limitations of performance ratings as you consider the role they play in the analytics you provide your organization.

Take a Deeper Dive

Read Lunenburg's "Performance Appraisal: Methods and Rating Errors."[8]

 Key Takeaways

- Before beginning any data analytics, always look at your data first. Are there any red flags? Does anything seem abnormal? It's important to address any issues with the data before moving forward.
- Descriptive statistics are a handy way of summarizing the data you have. They provide you with an overall sense of what you're working with. Be sure to look at measures of central tendency *and* variability to have a more thorough understanding of the information before you analyze your data.
- Your work is rarely finished after initial examinations of a hypothesis. It's unlikely that you'll clearly support or refute a hypothesis with your first few analyses. Be prepared to take a step back, brainstorm further analyses, and collect more data.

US Customs and Border Protection Uses Dashboards to Help Managers Track Skills

US Customs and Border Protection (CBP) is a government agency with an important mission: to safeguard America's borders while enhancing the nation's global economic competitiveness by enabling legitimate trade and travel. CBP needed a way to ensure that the agency's employees had the skills needed to be successful in their jobs, grow in their careers, and support the mission. They launched the Human Resources Management (HRM) Skills Assessment Tool (hereafter called "the Tool") in 2014, and relaunched it in 2016 as part of the ongoing strategy to meet that need.

The Tool is an online survey designed to assess key technical and general proficiency levels and training needs for HRM's largest occupational series. Employees provide self-ratings on proficiency and training needs in technical and general skill areas. Supervisors are also asked to provide proficiency and training-need ratings for each of their direct reports. The information collected by the Tool is used to

- meet requirements of the US Office of Personnel Management (OPM) and the Department of Homeland Security (DHS) to assess and address skill gaps;
- determine the type and level of training needed by HRM employees; and
- establish a skill set dashboard for HR's upper management to use in identifying trends and potential sources of skill reinforcement.

The 2016 version of the Tool was introduced to employees via an email from the assistant commissioner of HRM. Although completion of the Tool was voluntary, HRM employees were strongly encouraged to participate, resulting in a very high response rate (77 percent of HRM employees completed the assessment and 66 percent of HRM supervisors completed assessments for their direct reports).

Each CBP employee who completes the Tool receives a Skills Overview Assessment Report (SOAR) containing his or her self-ratings, the ratings made by that employee's supervisors (if available), a comparison between the two sets of ratings, and developmental feedback where applicable. Each SOAR also contains a skills-to-training crosswalk between the technical and general skill areas assessed by the Tool, currently available no-cost training, and other resources.

Each supervisor who provides ratings for his or her direct reports receives a SOAR for Supervisors (SOAR-S) containing the ratings a supervisor made for a given direct report, as well as the skills-to-training crosswalk. Supervisors also receive a SOAR-S user guide, which provides a framework and expectations for the supervisor's role in the employee development process, including an overview of how to utilize the SOAR reports for employee development and guidance on leading developmental discussions.

The results of the Tool are also aggregated into a dashboard (Figure 5.6) available to all HRM supervisors. The dashboard provides summaries of employees' proficiency and training needs in HRM's technical and general skill areas in an interactive, graphic format. The dashboard also offers a summary of critical skill gaps (defined as an employee having little or no proficiency and a high training need; Figure 5.7).

Recent results from the Federal Employee Viewpoint Survey (FEVS) indicate that the Tool may be contributing to a score increase on the question, "My training needs are assessed." Scores for this question have risen approximately 10 percent since the Tool was first launched.

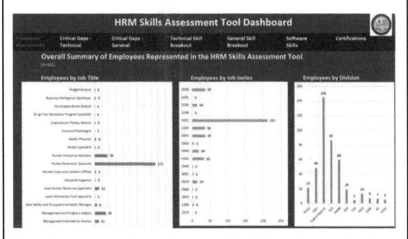

Figure 5.6. Customs & Border Protection HRM Skills Assessment Tool Dashboard: Overall Summary

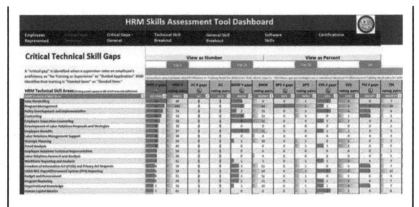

Figure 5.7. Customs & Border Protection HRM Skills Assessment Tool Dashboard: Critical Technical Skill Gaps

Endnotes

1. Aarti Gupta et al., *The Ultimate Guide to Basic Data Cleaning* (SocialCops, 2017), https://cdn2.hubspot.net/hubfs/2287011/ebook_data_cleaning/ Free%20Ebook%20-%20The%20Ultimate%20Guide%20to%20Basic%20 Data%20Cleaning.pdf.

2. David M. Lane, "Normal Distribution," in *HyperStat Online: An Introductory Statistics Textbook*, last modified March 1, 2008, http:// davidmlane.com/hyperstat/normal_distribution.html.

3. Kyle Maclean, Lauren E. Cipriano, and Gregory S. Zaric, "Descriptive Statistics in Microsoft Excel," *Harvard Business Review*, June 29, 2016.

4. Walter C. Borman, "Consistency of Rating Accuracy and Rating Errors in the Judgment of Human Performance," *Organizational Behavior and Human Performance* 20, no. 2 (1977): 238–52.

5. Edward L. Thorndike, "A Constant Error in Psychological Ratings," *Journal of Applied Psychology* 4, no. 1 (1920): 25–29.

6. C. Allen Gorman and Joan R. Rentsch, "Evaluating Frame-of-Reference Rater Training Effectiveness Using Performance Schema Accuracy," *Journal of Applied Psychology* 94, no. 5 (2009): 1336–44.

7. Robert M. Guion, *Assessment, Measurement, and Prediction for Personnel Decisions*, 2nd ed. (London: Routledge, 2011).

8. Fred C. Lunenburg, "Performance Appraisal: Methods and Rating Errors," *International Journal of Scholarly Academic Intellectual Diversity* 14, no. 1 (2012): 1–9.

6

Explore Complex Analyses

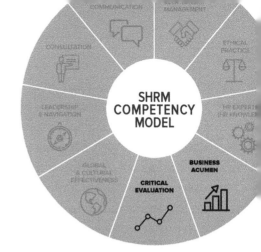

SHRM COMPETENCY MODEL

 Chapter Snapshot

Questions we will answer:

- What analytics can I run if I want to determine whether there is a relationship between two or more variables?
- What type of analysis can I run if I want to make a prediction?
- How can I assess differences between different groups of employees?

When we left Jen in Chapter 5, she had reviewed multiple data sources to better understand what's causing turnover in R&D. Unfortunately, different sources are pointing to different causes and she still doesn't have evidence to support that pay is the cause or that the top performers are the ones leaving. Let's check in and see how she decides to push on.

....

Jen has already looked at the engagement data. But is there more story to tell? Maybe there's something else in the data that she should take a closer look at. She thinks back to what the organizational effectiveness specialist said about turnover intent. In the engagement survey, employees are asked to indicate how likely they are to leave the company in the next twelve months. Perhaps there are other factors that are strongly related to that? How can Jen figure that out? She asks an analyst to run some correlations with the "likelihood of leaving" data. Now she'll need to know what to look for when the analyst comes back with the results.

....

On their own, descriptive statistics tell you relatively little about any HR problem. They're a good starting point, but more than likely you'll need to explore relationships among key variables. Just looking at turnover intent scores won't tell Jen a whole lot. She needs to understand where those scores fit into the bigger picture. Do employees who say they're more likely to leave follow through? That is, is it related to actual turnover? What are the things that lead employees to want to leave the organization? This is where relationships come into play. Examining relationships can be especially useful in looking toward the future. Often, relationships can help you predict future outcomes.

Before looking into relationships, you'll need to identify your criterion and predictor variables. A *criterion variable* is the outcome of interest. *Predictor variables* are those that help predict or explain the outcome. Your problem or hypothesis can guide you in this. In Jen's case, turnover and turnover intent would be criterion variables because she wants to know why people are leaving or planning to leave R&D. Things like salary, performance, and engagement would be predictor variables because those are the things Jen and her team think might help them understand who is leaving.

Often, you'll want to start examining relationships by looking at some correlations. A *correlation* is a measure of the linear relationship between two variables. If you were interested in looking at the relationship between grades in a training course and employee performance ratings, you'd want to know the correlation. A correlation analysis produces a single number: the correlation coefficient. Correlation coefficients can range from −1 to 1. This number tells you (a) how strong the relationship is, and (b) what direction the relationship is in. In statistics, correlation coefficients are abbreviated as "r." If you're looking at results from an analysis, look for "$r =$" followed by a number. That number is your correlation coefficient.

The numeric value of the correlation coefficient reveals how strong the relationship is. Numbers closer to zero tell you that the relationship is relatively weak. A correlation of zero indicates that there is no linear relationship between the two variables. As the coefficient approaches one or negative one, the relationship gets stronger. If you see a correlation coefficient of 1 or –1, this means there is a perfect linear relationship. The stronger the relationship between two variables, the better the prediction you're able to make from one variable to another. For example, if the correlation between turnover intent and actual turnover in R&D were 0.77, Jen could make reasonably strong predictions about an employee's likelihood of leaving based on his or her turnover intent score.

The sign of the correlation coefficient tells you the direction of the relationship. If the coefficient is negative, this means there is an inverse relationship: as one variable increases, the other decreases. You might expect a negative correlation between job satisfaction and voluntary turnover. The higher job satisfaction is, the lower the rate of quitting will likely be. On the other hand, a positive correlation indicates a positive relationship. This means that both variables change in the same direction. You might expect to see a positive correlation between tenure and salary. The longer someone has been employed with a company, the higher their salary is likely to be.

Correlations are easy to visualize when you graph your data. A *scatterplot* is a graph that plots all of your scores on two variables. The name tells you its intent: it's a graph that shows how scattered your data are. Each dot in a scatterplot represents an individual. If you have a scatterplot with fifty dots, there are fifty employees in your dataset. To better gauge the relationship between your two variables, look for a linear pattern among the dots. How closely do your data resemble a straight line? The closer the data points cluster in a line, the stronger the relationship is. The direction of this line also tells you the direction of the relationship. You read scatterplots left to right. If the line rises, the correlation is positive. If the line falls, you have a negative—or inverse—relationship. Figure 6.1 illustrates this for you.

....

Jen's team has the "pay" hypothesis they're testing, but they're considering some alternate hypotheses too. Jen asks the analyst to take a look at some other variables, specifically some variables from the engagement survey. The analyst comes back with the results in Table 6.1.

....

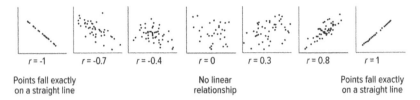

$r = -1$ $r = -0.7$ $r = -0.4$ $r = 0$ $r = 0.3$ $r = 0.8$ $r = 1$

Points fall exactly
on a straight line   No linear
relationship   Points fall exactly
on a straight line

Figure 6.1. Scatterplots of various correlation coefficients

Table 6.1. Correlations with likelihood of leaving

	Relationship with Supervisor	Recognition	Satisfaction with Pay
Turnover Intent	−0.234*	−0.395*	−0.208

*Statistically significant

> **Reflection**
>
> Look at the Table 6.1. How would you describe the relationship between turnover intent and (a) relationship with supervisor, (b) recognition, and (c) satisfaction with pay? What might this mean for the folks in R&D?
>
> _____
>
> _____
>
> _____
>
> _____
>
> _____

Look again at Table 6.1. When you compare this to the scatterplots in Figure 6.1, you might be tempted to say there aren't any meaningful relationships with turnover intent. It's true that correlation coefficients of 0.8 and 0.9 reflect very strong relationships. But those kinds of numbers _rarely_ happen with real HR data. A meaningful relationship among common HR variables will likely fall within the 0.25–0.40 range.

A useful way of gauging relationships among variables is looking for statistical significance. _Statistical significance_ indicates that it's unlikely your finding was due to chance. It can be thought of as a probability statement. If a relationship is significant at the 5 percent level (or a probability of 0.05), then that relationship would be expected to occur only five times out of one hundred as the result of chance alone. The problem with statistical significance is that it's sensitive to sample size. In other words, if enough people are included in your dataset, even very small relationships will be statistically significant. In HR, we often have the opposite problem. We don't typically have data from huge groups of people. Statistical significance also tells you nothing about the strength of a relationship or its meaning.

More often than not, you should be looking for *practical significance*. Practical significance asks the question, Is the relationship strong enough to have real meaning? It's likely your results reflect a real relationship. To gauge this, there's a rule of thumb in the behavioral sciences:[1]

- Weak relationships: $r \leq 0.10$
- Medium relationships: $0.10 < r < 0.50$
- Strong relationships: $r \geq 0.50$

Notice that two relationships in Table 6.1 are statistically significant: turnover intent with relationship with supervisor, and turnover intent with recognition. Does this mean the relationship between turnover intent and satisfaction with pay isn't important? Not necessarily. If you think about practical significance, it wouldn't be wise to dismiss this relationship.

 Take a Deeper Dive

Take a look at Gallo's "A Refresher on Statistical Significance."[2]

Correlations are a good way to start exploring relationships. But what do you do if you're interested in more than two variables? After all, the workplace is complex. Many forces are operating at once. If you're trying to explain something like turnover, it's unlikely one variable is solely responsible. It makes sense to explore the role of multiple variables at once. With more than one predictor, you may be able to make more accurate predictions about your criterion. However, things will also get more complicated. It's quite likely your predictor variables will be related to each other as well as to the criterion. Figure 6.2 illustrates this. You can think of a correlation like a simple Venn diagram. The amount of overlap between the two variables represents the relationship or association between them. When you add more predictors into the picture, things start to look like the image on the right of Figure 6.2.

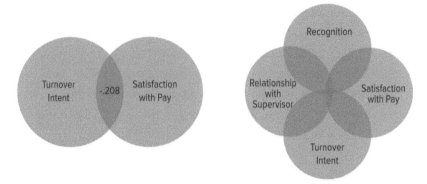

Figure 6.2. Correlation vs. Multiple Regression

To look at multiple predictors at once, you can use *multiple regression.* Multiple regression is a way of identifying the relationship between one criterion variable and multiple predictors. Similar to correlations, multiple regression gives you a summary number that tells you how strong the relationship is between all predictor variables and the criterion. Recall that this coefficient is r for correlations. It's represented by R for regressions. This analysis also provides a mathematical equation that allows you to predict the criterion in the future.

Take a Deeper Dive
Check out "Statisticians Don't Need a Crystal Ball to Predict the Future" by the American Statistical Association.[3]

Let's say Jen's analyst took the data a step further and followed up the correlations in Table 6.1 with a multiple regression. Turnover intent is the outcome Jen is trying to understand, so that will be her criterion variable. All other variables are predictors. The resulting information would tell Jen how relationship with supervisor, recognition, and satisfaction with pay jointly predict likelihood of leaving. As with correlations, both statistical and practical significance should be taken into account here. Practical significance can be taken from a measure of effect size. In multiple regression, a common measure of effect size is R^2. There are also rules of thumb here:[4]

- Small effect: $R^2 \leq 0.02$
- Medium effect: $0.02 < R^2 < 0.26$
- Large effect: $R^2 \geq 0.26$.

The fundamentals of regression can get pretty technical. If you'd like to better understand how regression works and what the actual results look like, take a look at the Deeper Dive section below.

Take a Deeper Dive

Gallo wrote "A Refresher on Regression Analysis" for readers who want to know more.[5] There is also *Applied Regression: An Introduction* by Colin and Michael Lewis-Beck.[6]

Jen's team is moving along nicely now. They're building a solid understanding of the factors that drive turnover intent. But Jen wants to make sure they maintain a focus on the employees who actually left R&D. What if the people who left and the people who stayed aren't really comparable? How can they ensure that the insights they're gathering based on people who are still with the organization will really help them understand the people who left? If they don't take a comprehensive look at the R&D separations, they might misdiagnose the problem. The team discusses how they might compare their turnover intent findings to the data they have on actual separations.

Jen is expressing interest in comparing two groups: current employees and those who have separated. This requires making some mean (average) comparisons. These kinds of analyses determine how different the means of two groups are. Are they different enough to conclude that the two groups are in fact different on some variable? Let's think back to performance ratings in R&D. In the last chapter, Jen's team looked at frequency distributions for performance scores of recent separations and the rest of the department (Table 5.4). A frequency distribution may offer a quick glance at how similar these two groups are, but it's hard to make concrete conclusions from that table. If she used a mean comparison to better understand the two groups, she'd get a clearer sense of how similar or different they really are. A t-*test* is a common method for comparing the means of two groups. When a *t*-test is conducted, a *t*-statistic will be computed. Like *r* and *R*, the *t*-value may or may not be statistically significant. As with multiple regression, you can look to measures of effect size to gauge practical significance. Cohen's *d* is the effect size most commonly associated with *t*-tests. It is associated with its own rules of thumb:[7]

- Small effect: $d \leq 0.20$
- Medium effect: $0.20 < d < 0.80$
- Large effect: $d \geq 0.80$

You may be wondering why you need to perform a special test just to compare two means. Couldn't you just look at the means and gauge how different they are? Well, not exactly. Recall what I told you about central tendency and variability in the last chapter. Those concepts work best together. This is exactly what a *t*-test does. It takes both central tendency—the mean for each group—and variability into account to give you a more accurate sense of the groups and how they compare. Figure 6.3 helps illustrate this by showing you a *t*-test comparing groups with different levels of variability.

....

Jen asks the analyst to perform some t-*tests to compare the separations with current employees. Thinking about her conversations with management, she wants the analyst to see how the groups differ on pay and performance. Are the separations truly top performers? Is their pay worse?*

The analyst comes back with very small effect sizes for both pay and performance. The t-*tests weren't statistically significant either. This doesn't provide great initial support for the managers' hypothesis, or for their claims that their best people are leaving. But this isn't bad news. The fact that recent*

separations and current R&D employees appear to be fairly similar on pay and
performance means Jen can work with the people still working in R&D. She
and her team start brainstorming ways to make use of the employees they have
to get to the bottom of things.

Jen and her team continue to unpack the situation in R&D. The
analytic process is iterative. At each juncture, HR analysts must evaluate
the assumptions being made and test them to make sure they hold up.
In Jen's story, the team tested the managers' assumptions (that the best
performers are leaving because of pay) and also their own (that current
employees can help them understand former employees). It's important to
take notice of the assumptions being made (including your own!) and be
willing to test them. It's not just good science—it's good business.

In the next chapter, Jen and her team will explore additional ways
to turn the effect sizes and significance tests into a story. This will again
involve integrating additional data sources from within and outside the
organization—and not all of it is quantitative. Jen will also work to piece it
all together. Understanding the problem is a great first step. She'll need to
tackle figuring out what to do about it to really demonstrate value.

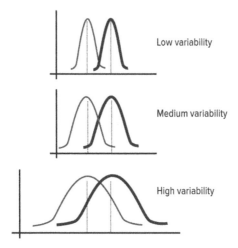

Figure 6.3. Mean comparisons via *t*-tests across different levels of variability
Note: Areas of overlap between the two curves indicate areas where the two groups do
not differ.

How Might This Look Different in Small Organizations?

At the beginning of this book, I talked a bit about small organizations and how HR analytics might differ for them. Small organizations have fewer employees overall, so you'll be collecting less data. Smaller data sets don't lend themselves to robust analyses, so this may impact the level in the HR analytics hierarchy at which you operate. It may also mean you need to get creative. Perhaps your organization doesn't have the resources to regularly conduct exit interviews, engagement surveys, and the like. Can you collect some of this data on your own? Leaning more heavily on qualitative data will give you depth where you lack breadth. Are there other ways to fill any gaps? External data sources—things like benchmarking and published research studies—may become some of your new closest friends. Some human friendships can go a long way too! There are plenty of online communities on sites like LinkedIn (Linked:HR is especially active). These are great avenues to post questions and learn from others.

Smaller organizations usually mean small HR departments. Perhaps you're an HR department of one? In these instances it's unlikely you have the luxury of dedicated analysts. One possible solution is outsourcing. Hiring interns or part-time graduate students with statistics chops may give you the boost you need. That may be too expensive, so a more local alternative is to look in-house. Business elements such as IT or engineering may have the expertise you're after, and forming partnerships with them could go a long way. It's also possible that you'll have to integrate some analytics into your own repertoire. If you happen to be a department of one, you might feel like you just don't have the time for analytics. However, analytics are even more critical in these cases. It can help you determine where your time is best spent. Are you solving the right problems? The Deeper Dives I've given you so far, as well as the resources in the appendices, provide some support for boosting your own statistical repertoire.

 From the SHRM Research Lab

Think about the last time you made an important decision, like whether to stay at your job or to seek a new opportunity. What factors were at play? You may have consciously weighed factors such as your pay, benefits, coworkers, commute, advancement opportunities, and how much you liked your boss. There were probably other factors that you weren't even conscious of—for example, how risk-averse you tend to be and macroeconomic factors.

The behavioral sciences are commonly referred to as the "soft sciences." Compared to disciplines like physics and chemistry—"hard sciences"—there's less objectivity in measurement in behavioral science. Human behavior is incredibly complex. It's influenced by personality traits, biological characteristics, and social norms, among many other factors. Often this means that our methodologies must be even more rigorous. As HR works to increase the role of analytics, academic researchers are working to expand the analytic toolkit at our disposal. A multitude of advanced analyses exist to help us cope with the complexity of human behavior.

Catastrophic models are one example of complex analytical approaches that are gaining traction in our field. These models describe discontinuous phenomena: things that involve a sudden, catastrophic change.[8] This kind of pattern has been observed in the context of physical labor. For instance, research studying steel mill workers involved measuring arm strength before and after two hours of strenuous labor. After working for two hours, some employees showed a sharp decrease in strength—likely the result of fatigue—while others showed an increase, as if they'd just been warming up for the past two hours.[9]

Random coefficient models are another advanced approach to capturing the complexity of human behavior. These models allow you to look at time-varying predictor models.[10] Essentially, how does a change in one variable predict a change in another? For example, how do changes in knowledge acquisition relate to changes in job performance over time?

Social network analysis is also gaining popularity of late. This approach is used to model social influence and communication within organizational contexts. The kinds of analyses I've described in this book tend to simplify interpersonal relationships. Social network analysis treats individuals as interdependent and accounts for those interconnected relationships. Data can be depicted in the form of a web or matrix to display the interdependencies.[11] This approach can be a handy way to study emergent leaders in an organization. What are the characteristics and situations that tend to give rise to leadership? That kind of information can be helpful for a range of organizational purposes. Wouldn't it be nice to know which of your individual contributors carries influence with a large number of their peers before your next change initiative?

These techniques, and many others, use mathematical rigor to help us understand something as convoluted as human behavior as precisely as possible. As organizations begin to routinize data collection, aggregation, cleaning, and reporting, time and space are freed up to focus on more complex questions. Your organization might not be ready for random modeling yet, but it's never too soon to start imagining how you might apply advanced techniques to your most perplexing people challenges.

 Key Takeaways

- Correlations are a great starting point for uncovering relationships between variables. A correlation allows you to measure the strength of a linear relationship between two variables—a predictor and a criterion.
- Multiple regression also allows you to explore relationships and make predictions. However, multiple regression analyses give you the ability to test how multiple variables predict an outcome of interest.
- You may not always be interested in testing relationships. You might want to look at how one group of employees differs from another. This can be done with means comparisons such as t-tests.

A Multinational Consulting Firm Uses Analytics to Improve Diversity

Organizations with greater diversity among their leaders often outperform organizations with less diversity. With this in mind, multinational consulting firm FTI Consulting decided to proactively set goals to increase the representation of women in senior leadership positions. The dilemma was how to set aggressive but realistic goals. The ratio of female leaders to male leaders is affected by many factors, including turnover, hiring, and promotions. The chief human capital officer tasked the talent analytics team to analyze several years of data and apply scenario modeling to answer two questions: What is a realistic goal for the firm by 2020? and, What types of interventions would be most effective to achieve this goal?

The analytics team started by gathering several years of turnover, hiring, and promotion data, and the current headcount. They structured the data so that rosters of person-level data with all the necessary demographics and job data were linked to pivot tables (tables that summarize data in another table) of counts and percentages by gender, job level, and year. Using those tables and the what-if analysis tool in Excel, the team created scenarios extrapolating trends in the historic data out to 2020.

A status quo model applied historic trends in turnover, hiring, and promotions to the current headcount, showing how the ratio of female senior leaders to male senior leaders would change each year from 2016 through 2020. Three other models showed the effect of decreasing female turnover, increasing female hiring, or increasing female promotions. These scenarios revealed that even modest reductions in female turnover would have more of an impact than large changes to hiring and promotions. Not surprisingly, other scenarios revealed that addressing all three levers (turnover, hiring, and promotions) would lead to better outcomes. The trend analysis and scenario modeling helped the team identify problematic trends for specific business units and job levels, and what types of HR interventions would have the largest impact for each business unit.

Figure 6.4 shows five scenarios. The status quo shows the number of female leaders trending up from 2016 to 2020 given historic trends. Other scenarios—especially reducing turnover or taking a comprehensive approach to hire, promote, and retain— would significantly increase the number of female leaders and the ratio of female leaders to male leaders.

The end results of the analysis were aggressive but realistic goals for each business unit that senior leaders agreed to adopt; trend reports highlighting problem areas (e.g., high turnover at specific job levels); and recommendations for retention, hiring, and promotion strategies. Strategies for retention were bolstered by additional analyses of employee engagement and exit surveys, and by highlighting specific areas for HR and business partners to address.

The firm continues to use analytics to track progress against those goals and is seeing positive results. The analytics team updates the models with new data at least once per year to inform senior leaders whether current strategies are working or if more aggressive action is needed. This program will continue to inform the business well beyond 2020.

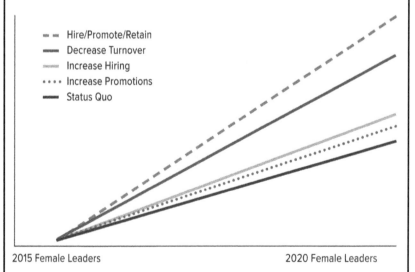

- – Hire/Promote/Retain
- — Decrease Turnover
- Increase Hiring
- •••• Increase Promotions
- — Status Quo

2015 Female Leaders   2020 Female Leaders

Figure 6.4. FTI scenarios to increase representation of women in leadership

Endnotes

1. Jacob Cohen, *Statistical Power Analysis for the Behavioral Sciences*, 2nd ed. (Hillsdale, NJ: Lawrence Erlbaum, 1988).
2. Amy Gallo, "A Refresher on Statistical Significance," *Harvard Business Review*, February 16, 2016, https://hbr.org/2016/02/a-refresher-on-statistical-significance.
3. American Statistical Association, "Statisticians Don't Need a Crystal Ball to Predict the Future," ThisIsStatistics.org, April 28, 2016, http://thisisstatistics.org/statisticians-dont-need-a-crystal-ball-to-predict-the-future/.
4. Cohen, *Statistical Power Analysis*.
5. Amy Gallo, "A Refresher on Regression Analysis," *Harvard Business Review*, November 4, 2015, https://hbr.org/2015/11/a-refresher-on-regression-analysis.
6. Colin Lewis-Beck and Michael Lewis-Beck, *Applied Regression: An Introduction*, 2nd ed. (Newbury Park, CA: Sage Publications, 2016).
7. Cohen, *Statistical Power Analysis*.
8. Stephen J. Guastello et al., "Cusp Catastrophe Models for Cognitive Workload and Fatigue: A Comparison of Seven Task Types," *Nonlinear Dynamics, Psychology, and Life Sciences* 17, no. 1 (2013): 23–47.
9. Stephen J. Guastello and David W. McGee, "Mathematical Modeling of Fatigue in Physically Demanding Jobs," *Journal of Mathematical Psychology* 31, no. 3 (1987): 248–69.
10. Robert Ployhart and Youngsang Kim, "Dynamic Longitudinal Growth Modeling," in *Modern Research Methods for the Study of Behavior in Organizations*, ed. Jose M. Cortina and Ronald S. Landis (London: Routledge, 2014), 63–98.
11. Yuval Kalish, "Harnessing the Power of Social Network Analysis to Explain Organizational Phenomena," in *Modern Research Methods*, 99–135.

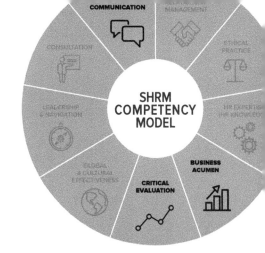

7

Use Data to Inform Your Decisions

Chapter Snapshot
Questions we will answer:

- How can I better understand the quantitative results I'm seeing?
- How can I use what I've learned from the analytics to make decisions about organizational interventions?
- Where can I use evidence from outside of my organization to help me?

Recall where Jen's team left off in Chapter 6. Jen had just discovered that the employees who recently left R&D did not differ substantially from current employees on pay or performance. This led Jen to want to look more closely at the people still employed with R&D.

....

Jen wants to look at more data—how about focus groups or stay interviews? The team needs to learn more about the managers too. Why aren't they using the tools available to them? Jen decides to start by talking to the managers. She wants to learn more from them, but also get their buy-in for talking to the employees. The HR business partner (HRBP) joins Jen when she meets with the managers again.

....

Reflection

Why is it important for Jen to get manager buy-in before talking to employees?

_____

_____

_____

....

Jen provides the managers with a brief update on the actions she's been taking. Then she asks permission to ask them some additional questions to better understand what's going on. She starts by reviewing her understanding of the challenge and specifically mentions the last few separations. First, Jen asks about the impact this has had on the managers' business objectives. They talk about having to scale back their commitments. They say they just don't have enough people to get it all done and are spending their own time trying to help recruit and hire, without much luck.

....

Jen made a great call in seeking a follow-up meeting with management. First, collecting new data is often required to really understand what's going on. Too often, people stop with the data they have on hand. That can mean making decisions based on pretty limited data that weren't necessarily collected with your challenge in mind. Beyond the data, that meeting gives her the chance to learn more about the situation and also accomplishes some other things.

Touching base again with the managers lets them know that Jen is prioritizing their problem. Taking an approach like this will allow you to maintain a closed loop of communication with your stakeholders; no one is left wondering what's being done. Checking in with your stakeholders also gives you more practice speaking their language. You'll get an even better sense of what variables are important to them, and how they define and talk about those variables. This way, when you present your findings to them later, you can frame things in a way that resonates with them.

In Jen's situation, she's not just trying to learn more about management's perspective; she's seeking their buy-in for conducting stay interviews. Carrying out the stay interviews will require additional resources, and she'll be taking employees away from their work to meet with them. There may be additional funds and resources needed to then work with the interview data. Any time you're looking to collect additional data, some level of added resources will be required. Obtaining stakeholder buy-in for this can help you make the best business case for expending resources on your data collection. Talking to your stakeholders will give you a better sense of how your data can impact the bottom line.

....

The managers also mention that they're having to spend more time with the rest of the staff since the people who left were informal leaders and were technically strong. Jen asks more about that. She can tell how important these people were to the organization. She wants to learn more about what they know about why these employees left. Did they see it coming? What was done to try and keep them before they resigned? What about after they resigned?

Through the conversation, Jen learns that management characterizes the culture in R&D as high performing. They try to be very selective about whom they bring in. Everyone is really smart and hardworking. They don't give out a lot of awards because the expectation is that everyone is going above and beyond every day.

Jen takes the opportunity to point out that their personnel files made it hard to identify the recent separations as high potentials on paper. The managers look at each other a bit uncomfortably and say that if they were going to reward people, they'd have to reward everyone and there just isn't a budget for that. That's part of the reason they just need to be able to pay more. "What about developmental opportunities or other options?" Jen asks. The managers say they'd been concerned about creating feelings of inequity.

....

Reflection

Think about Jen's conversation with the managers. Other than performance ratings or rewards, how else might they identify high performers?

_____

_____

_____

In a perfect world, Jen would have data to verify or call into question the managers' claims that the employees who are leaving are top performers. She has no such data. But can she find it somewhere else? It's possible. Things like being identified in a succession plan, number of projects completed, and even the criteria used during hiring might prove useful.

....

The managers agree to let Jen's team conduct some focus groups and interviews with the employees. But they remind her that they're looking for a pay proposal. She thanks them for their time and heads back to her office to debrief with the HRBP.

Jen asks the HRBP what she heard. "It sounds like pay may not be the only problem," the HRBP responds. She goes on to say that she wonders whether the departing employees even know how their managers perceived them. There seems to be conflicting information here—either everyone is great or there are a few people who are disproportionately great and they're leaving. The HRBP speculates that pay may be an easy win for the team—they already know how to fix it. No one will complain about more pay, and there's little additional burden on the managers with a fair amount of potential upside.

Jen agrees that all of this is reasonable but reminds her to hold it loosely. They now have at least two competing hypotheses for why people are leaving: (a) too little pay, or (b) too little recognition and development. They have to make sure to let the data tell the story. It's time to interview the employees.

....

Remember that data collection isn't a one-and-done task. Don't let this discourage you. You're only strengthening your arguments with more data collection. In Jen's case, the R&D managers are clearly displaying their bias toward the pay hypothesis. In situations like this it can be tough to continue looking for clues. But in HR, it's important for us to make data-driven decisions. The R&D organization wouldn't launch a new product without testing it first to make sure it works, and HR shouldn't launch changes to the human capital system without research either. What has the research shown so far, and where are there holes?

....

After meeting with the managers and hearing what they had to say, Jen felt pretty comfortable that she had two competing hypotheses. First, that people were leaving because the company isn't paying enough and if they start paying more, people will stay. Alternatively, that people are leaving because they're uncertain what good performance looks like, where they stand, and how to advance. Pay might be part of the issue, but a pay increase by itself wouldn't solve the problem.

Before Jen starts scheduling interviews and focus groups, she wants to review what she's learned from all the data so far. She starts compiling all of her findings (see Table 7.1).

....

Table 7.1. Summary of R&D data

Data Set	Findings
Engagement Scores	Overall, R&D engagement scores aren't great, they're • higher than the company average for meaningfulness of work and regard for colleagues, and • lower than average for management and supervision, and awards and recognition. Employees believe they can be paid more elsewhere. Recognition is more strongly related to turnover intent than salary is.
Performance Scores	The people leaving don't look like top performers. Performance ratings weren't much higher than average for those who left. There is no pattern of awards or recognition for employees who have left the organization.
Exit Interviews	People mentioned opportunities for development or growth as often as they mentioned salary.
Compensation Data	The company pays above the median in the market, at about the 65th percentile. On average, the R&D employees who left were more likely to have been paid below the median within the pay range. The salary increases of separated employees were consistently modest over time and were not systematically higher than those of employees who stayed.
Recruiting Data	Data quality and integrity issues prevented us from being able to assess how frequently applicants were turning down offers for salary reasons.

Reflection

Think about Jen's findings above. Use the table below and indicate what each data source points to as the root cause of turnover based on what we know thus far.

Data Set	Root Cause of Turnover
Engagement Scores	
Performance Scores	
Exit Interviews	
Compensation Data	
Recruiting Data	

No data source is perfect. Every person you talk to at work has a different perspective, and so does every data source. That's why it's so important to look at a problem from multiple angles. Doing so can help overcome the limitations of any single source, and it ensures you aren't missing anything.

Jen's team is making use of both current survey data and *archival data*. Archival data are any pieces of information collected before your research begins. In Jen's case, the recruitment data is one example of archival data. Survey and archival data can help you understand what happened and what employees think. Discussions with employees can help you understand *why*. For example, we know from the engagement survey (one of our archival data sources) that the R&D employees are less satisfied with rewards and recognition and management than other aspects of their jobs. What we don't know is why. Jen's team has some guesses based on what they're seeing from personnel files, but focus groups and stay interviews can be a good opportunity to see if those guesses are supported.

Again, nothing is perfect. There is a downside to focus groups and interviews: they're time-consuming to conduct. Once you've made a survey, you can send it out and get back to other parts of your job. This isn't true of employee discussions. It might also be difficult to generalize your findings from them, depending on how many interviews you do and how employees are chosen. If Jen only conducted interviews with direct reports of one supervisor, it would be hard to generalize her findings to the rest of R&D management.

Given time and resource constraints, it's important to make the most of your discussion time. In Jen's case, she can't cover all the topics included in the engagement survey or the other data sources her team has. She needs to make sure she focuses the discussion on the areas where the *why* is most likely to be helpful. Open-ended questions are best for getting the conversation flowing. In focus groups, they can also help encourage interaction between participants. Make sure you're setting participants up to give you detailed explanations; for example, "Would you say you're likely to stay with our company for the next few years?" is likely to elicit a one- or two-word response. Also, general questions tend to elicit general answers. You'll want to make sure to ask specific questions about topics of interest. Instead of asking, "How satisfied are you with your work?" you may want to inquire about specific areas of interest to you. For example, you could instead ask, "What elements of your job do you find most meaningful?"

 Take a Deeper Dive

The SHRM article "How to Conduct an Employee Focus Group" in their online how-to guides is beneficial for further reading.[1]

Reflection

Given what Jen's team has found so far, what would you want to ask the employees? How could you use their responses to fill in the rest of the story?

_____

_____

_____

_____

_____

_____

....

After reviewing what they've gotten so far in more detail, the team decides on an approach for the upcoming meetings. For the focus groups, Jen decides to start broad. She reviews the engagement results and asks employees what they think is driving the lower scores in specific areas. Then she asks specifically about management, pay, rewards and recognition, and professional development—all of the things that have emerged as issues thus far. In the stay interviews, Jen decides to ask employees what they like best about their jobs and what could be done to make them even better. She also decides to ask how they like to be recognized and what motivates them.

....

Take a Deeper Dive

The SHRM article "Stay Interview Questions" under their online HR forms is beneficial for further reading.[2]

....

Jen conducts the interviews and focus groups with help from the HRBP and the organizational effectiveness specialist. They learn that pay is among the issues, but it isn't a key driver. Multiple employees say that although they're contacted by recruiters who promise higher pay, they really enjoy their work right now. They value having the chance to create. They also love working with other smart, passionate people and having so much flexibility. Their managers let them set their own schedules and they get to choose how to execute tasks. But that's also part of the problem.

The managers are so hands-off that the employees don't really have a sense of whether they're on the right track. One of the managers has a reputation for being a bit aloof—even socially awkward. He engages in technical questions if the employees ask for help, but he doesn't give much career guidance or performance feedback. The other manager engages more, but was sometimes described as aggressive. It feels like nothing the employees do is good enough. More than one employee commented that they'd always been at the top of their class and were high performers at their previous jobs. Here, they get average ratings with no clear guidance for improving. They don't see a path for growth.

When the team asked what would keep them there, only one employee out of fifteen said higher pay. Despite all the employees having pretty comparable positions in the pay band, pay just wasn't showing up as a major concern. The others talked about developmental opportunities, better feedback and guidance, and clearer communication around what "good" looks like. Jen asked the employees whether they'd shared their feedback with the managers. Most simply said no, but a few suggested that the managers don't seem receptive.

The picture is becoming much clearer now. But Jen has the challenge of packaging all of this into a succinct and compelling message to present to the leadership team. Her goal is to explain the issues according to the evidence her team collected and convince leadership to partner with her on solutions. Going into the presentation saying they're the problem isn't a solution, it's an observation, and one they probably won't like. Jen calls the team back together to develop a game plan.

What's happening in Jen's scenario is not uncommon. Projects typically start because someone in your company is experiencing discomfort. The uncomfortable person then develops an explanation for the problem and possible solutions are pursued. The catch is that the solutions are unlikely to work if they're addressing the wrong problem.

Data analytics is a powerful tool to increase the likelihood that you have the right problem. Both quantitative and qualitative data serve a purpose in supporting a hypothesis. They allow you to objectively measure and identify patterns and relationships. Jen's team has gone through a few rounds of collecting and evaluating data to understand the situation. Now it's solution time. Before they identify a solution, though, they should redefine the problem to make sure the solution is aligned.

Take a Deeper Dive

Read "Are You Solving the Right Problem?" by Dwayne Spradlin.[3]

Reflection

How would you redefine the problem?

_____

_____

_____

_____

_____

....

Jen starts the next team meeting off with a short update on the discussions with the R&D team members. She then takes some time to redefine the problem based on what the team knows now. This started as a turnover problem with a relatively simple proposed solution: pay. It was also a pretty innocent one—no one in R&D had any direct responsibility for pay. Now there seem to be a few root causes.

Thinking about the managers, they mean well. They want to promote equity. This means they aren't using many of the tools available to them to differentially pay or recognize their high performers formally or informally. Despite that, they also acknowledge that some employees are contributing more to the business than others. Too bad those employees don't know that.

The managers sound like they fell into the same trap many technically oriented leaders fall into: they got to where they are now for their technical skills, but they don't have the same comfort level with the softer side of management. How can Jen help the managers see that career development and performance coaching are integral to creating a high-performing team and retaining star employees?

As far as the employees go, they love their work, their coworkers, and much about the environment. Pay may not be high enough to ward off more compelling offers, but it's really the lack of clarity that ultimately sways them. They don't know where they stand today or where they're going to be tomorrow within the company. That makes the affirmation they get from other suitors particularly appealing. How can these employees get more career development opportunities, coaching, and recognition so they're less susceptible to external offers?

The redefined problem requires a bit more accountability. Although no one in R&D has the sole authority to change pay, data analytics uncovered possible solutions that R&D leadership can directly impact.

....

Recall that in Chapter 2, I talked to you about evidence-based practice. Let's explore how Jen can use evidence-based practice to develop a proposal to improve the turnover situation for R&D.

There are four sources of information to rely on for evidence-based decisions. Jen's collected a lot of data to understand the organizational context. That's how her team has gotten where they are now. Based on those data, they have arrived at some key issues that need to be solved. But where do they go from there? How should they go about selecting an intervention? That's where the other sources come in.

Jen's team may not have a lot of data from within the company on the best way to develop leadership skills or motivate and recognize employees, but there's a world of information they can draw from. Academics and practitioners conduct studies across settings that provide useful insights. Those insights can be applied to Jen's situation and any situation you're dealing with in your own company. You can search for these kinds of studies through Google Scholar or through academic search engines like EBSCO.

Review articles, book chapters, and SHRM's Effective Practice Guidelines can be great places to get an overview. One thing to keep in mind is the quantity and quality of the evidence to support an intervention or practice. Refer to the guide at the end of this chapter for help evaluating this. I like to start by identifying the challenge, identifying potential interventions, and searching for evidence-based findings about that potential intervention to see if there is support, counterevidence, or both, and in what amounts. From there, you'll want to use your own professional judgment about what has worked in the past, your knowledge of your company's culture, and how you might tailor what you learned from the literature to your situation.

 Take a Deeper Dive

Consider reading Rousseau and Barends's "Becoming an Evidence-Based HR Practitioner," as well as watching "How to Google Like a Pro!" by Epic Tutorials for iOS & Android Filmmaking and "EBSCOhost Advanced Searching—Tutorial" by EBSCO Help.[4]

Jen decides to break down the current challenges and look for evidence on how to address each one. Table 7.2 shows what she found.

Jen and her team review the findings and discuss the best way to move forward. To solve this problem, they think they'll need a proposal with multiple

Table 7.2. Findings to support each R&D challenge

Challenge Employees Experience	Intervention	Evidence-Based Findings
Employees need more performance feedback, career coaching, and development opportunities.	Review the way the jobs and goals are constructed in the R&D organization. Look for opportunities to link employees' work to organizational goals so they see the impact of their work on the organization more directly. Look for opportunities to expand the responsibilities of the team members to cultivate new skills and knowledge and take advantage of development opportunities, including volunteering for special projects. Ensure that career paths exist and are being communicated.	Employees want job opportunities that facilitate growth and autonomy so they can feel like they have control over their environment.[5]
Employees want more recognition.	Have managers recognize the expertise of each employee and make assignments based on those. Emphasize the value of employee's ideas, even if they aren't put to an immediate use.	Recognition contributes to job satisfaction and has a positive impact on organizational productivity and performance.[6]
Employees are being approached by competitors who lead the market on pay.	Change pay target from 65th percentile to 75th percentile.	Although pay does not motivate employees to the extent many people believe, it is important to the extent that it helps employees satisfy their needs for security and autonomy.[7] Pay does, however, drive attraction and job choice.[8]

components. Pay is part of the proposal, but it won't address the whole problem by itself. Now that they've discussed what they think is necessary, the team needs to figure out what the company is already doing that they can leverage.

The HRBP isn't sure whether there's a clearly articulated career path for R&D employees. It may be that it doesn't exist, in which case, they'll need to develop it. Or it may be that it just isn't communicated clearly, which is something Jen can discuss with leadership.

In talking about the issues, the team also realizes that the managers have been in their roles for a while. They didn't go through the new manager training that the company built on performance management. Jen suggests inviting the managers to attend the next one or at least sharing the content with them in a more intimate setting. The team also discusses that they have a fairly new leader development program that was created for another part of the company. Conveniently, it was developed to help technical staff—engineers— in another area make the transition from individual contributor to manager. The program has been getting great reviews, so that may be a good option for the R&D leaders too. It doesn't currently have a coaching component, but that might be something to recommend as an add-on.

The team feels good about the proposal and is excited about the fact that there are opportunities to repurpose existing materials and programs.

Jen has gotten stakeholder input all along the way, but it's a good idea to get additional input once there's a proposal in place.

Notice that before creating anything new, the team thought about what they already had in place within their company. Was there anything already there that might meet their needs? Analytics can help you there too. You can use analytics to help you evaluate things you're already doing in your company. If those things are working well, you might want to extend them to other parts of the company. If they're not, analytics can help you identify what needs to be modified or discontinued before investing more resources.

Thinking along those lines, a company serves as an opportunity to run different "experiments" or pilot programs. Sometimes these happen intentionally or by design. Other times they occur naturally. For example, Jen could look at the engagement results to identify the departments with the highest scores. She could then seek out information about what those departments are doing differently in those areas. That can provide powerful internal examples to inspire new programs. It can also be a way to identify leaders who might be good mentors for others in the company.

Take a Deeper Dive

Take a look at one of Google's in-house experiments in "How Many Interviews Does It Take to Hire a Googler?" by Shannon Shaper.[13]

Jen finally has a comprehensive idea of what's going on in R&D. She also has a proposed solution to fix it. Next, she'll need to figure out how to explain all of that to her stakeholders and get agreement on the path forward. In Chapter 8, Jen will tackle that using storytelling and visualization to help her prepare her presentation to the stakeholders.

From the SHRM Research Lab

How can you motivate employees? Motivation is about energy, direction, and persistence. Organizations care a lot about motivating employees because it's a critical factor in performance. One of the most well-researched and supported theories of motivation is called *self-determination theory*.[14] This theory highlights the importance of feeling like you have control over your environment and can satisfy your basic human needs.[15] One way to remember these basic needs is the acronym CAMP:[16]

- **Community (or relatedness):** the need for belonging and attachment to others;
- **Autonomy:** the need to feel in control of one's own destiny (i.e., one's behaviors and goals);
- **Mastery (or competence):** the need to master tasks and learn new skills, as people want to be good at the work they do; and
- **Purpose:** the need to contribute to something bigger than oneself.

People can be motivated from within when they achieve a goal or accomplishment; this is called *intrinsic motivation*. Or, people can be motivated by an outside reward or demand; this is known as *extrinsic motivation*. Like the R&D managers in Jen's story, organizations often overestimate the role of money in motivating employees. Pay is an extrinsic motivator. These kinds of incentives have little impact on intrinsic motivation, and can even be detrimental to it.[17] Research suggests that intrinsic motivation is more powerful than extrinsic motivation, especially for sustained efforts.[18]

It isn't that pay doesn't matter—it does. It impacts people's attraction to a job and has relationships to other things that matter, such as security and status. But there are other, even more powerful ways to motivate people.[19] These include the characteristics of a job, such as the variety of tasks, feedback, recognition, responsibility, opportunities to develop new skills, opportunities to advance, and autonomy. Managers can help by looking for opportunities to enrich jobs or allow for some job crafting, where employees themselves can seek out projects or aspects of work that provide satisfaction.[20]

 Key Takeaways

- Analyzing survey and administrative data can help you understand what is happening. Interviews and focus groups can provide additional depth around why it's happening.
- Solutions are unlikely to succeed if they aren't addressing the right problem. The problem presented can often be misleading. Analytics are a powerful tool to help you assess and redefine the problem you're addressing.
- Combining information from your organizational context (based on what you learn from analytics) with information from external research can provide you with strong ground to stand on when you're designing an intervention.

BetterUp's Analytics Help Logitech Demonstrate Leadership Growth

Logitech's learning and development (L&D) team struggled to connect investments in learning to measurable behavior change. Impact had typically been limited to satisfaction surveys on whether people liked content and instructors. There had been little to no visibility into whether these investments were delivering impacts on business results, cultural goals, or company values.

Moreover, traditional learning programs weren't creating new behaviors that stuck. Even for the most motivated Logitech managers, workshop and classroom experiences led to small changes, but more often a quick return to the path of least resistance (i.e., doing things the old way.) Being inspired for one or two days simply wasn't enough to change their behavior in the long term.

Logitech recognized the issue and partnered with a third-party coaching vendor, BetterUp. The first thing BetterUp did was employ an evidence-based assessment to see where individual Logitech managers scored across twenty-six dimensions that research shows correlate to high performance and growth. Not only did these assessment results provide a baseline to later measure the progress of Logitech managers against their developmental goals, but they also enabled BetterUp to tailor its coaching to the specific needs of each individual.

Traditional approaches often miss a key ingredient for developing leaders: they neglect to address the internal resources that allow leaders to continuously learn, handle increased pressure, adapt to rapid change, and maintain high energy levels. Internal resources are the underpinning for lasting behavioral change. Without addressing them, Logitech's managers could model new leadership behaviors learned in a classroom for a few weeks. But if they hadn't learned how to manage stress or bounce back from setbacks, they would invariably revert back to their old behaviors.

This is why BetterUp developed a whole-person approach to leadership development. In partnership with its science board, BetterUp recognizes that people need to be in a place where they're thriving personally before they're able to truly inspire professionally.

In partnership with BetterUp, Logitech's L&D team was able to use analytics to provide clear evidence of stronger leaders to executive management. There were significant percentile improvements across key performance dimensions (Figure 7.1), increasing Logitech's scores for its company values of openness, humility, and challenge seeking:

- Levels of stress decreased by 23 percentile points and burnout decreased by 18 percentile points.
- Levels of hope improved by 15 percentile points and optimism improved by 13 percentile points.
- Logitech members had a 20 percentile point improvement against the national average, suggesting a positive impact on individuals' attitudes, behaviors, and performance.

These analytics provide a way for the L&D team to demonstrate the progress being made in Logitech's culture. Measuring the before and after scores on the whole-person assessment and combining them with the population-level effects from academic research allowed BetterUp to estimate Logitech's ROI in BetterUp coaching. By aggregating its gains in performance and retention with commensurate decreases in absences and healthcare spending, BetterUp conservatively predicted that Logitech's investment in BetterUp will yield a 4.3 ROI (Figure 7.2).

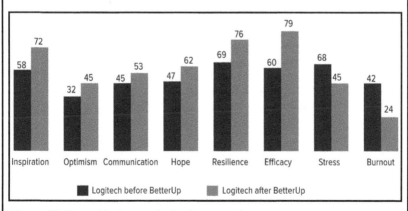

Figure 7.1. BetterUp Percentile Performance Improvements

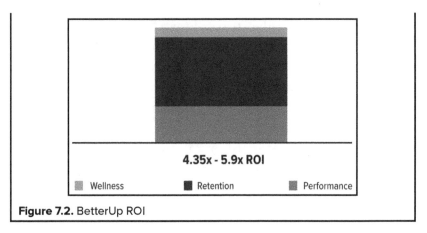

4.35x - 5.9x ROI

Wellness   Retention   Performance

Figure 7.2. BetterUp ROI

Endnotes

1. Society for Human Resource Management, "How to Conduct an Employee Focus Group," June 19, 2015, https://www.shrm.org/resourcesandtools/tools-and-samples/how-to-guides/pages/conduct-employee-focus-group.aspx.

2. Society for Human Resource Management, "Stay Interview Questions," accessed February 6, 2018, https://www.shrm.org/resourcesandtools/tools-and-samples/hr-forms/pages/stayinterviewquestions.aspx.

3. Dwayne Spradlin, "Are You Solving the Right Problem?," *Harvard Business Review*, September 2012, https://hbr.org/2012/09/are-you-solving-the-right-problem.

4. Denise M. Rousseau and Eric G. R. Barends, "Becoming an Evidence-Based HR Practitioner," *Human Resource Management Journal* 21, no. 3 (2011): 221–35, https://doi.org/10.1111/j.1748-8583.2011.00173.x; Epic Tutorials for iOS & Android Filmmaking, "How to Google Like a Pro! Top 10 Google Search Tips and Tricks," YouTube, April 5, 2010, https://youtu.be/R0DQfwc72PM; and EBSCO Help, "EBSCOhost Advanced Searching—Tutorial."

5. J. Richard Hackman and Greg R. Oldham, "Development of the Job Diagnostic Survey," *Journal of Applied Psychology* 60, no. 2 (1975): 159–170.

6. Steven H. Applebaum and Rammie Kamal, "An Analysis of the Utilization and Effectiveness of Non-financial Incentives in Small Business," *Journal of Management Development* 19, no. 9 (2000): 733–63.

7. Gary Latham, *Becoming the Evidence-Based Manager: Making the Science of Management Work for You* (Boston: Davies-Black, 2009).

8. Daniel M. Cable and Timothy A. Judge, "Pay Preferences and Job Search Decisions: A Person-Organization Fit Perspective," *Personnel Psychology* 47, no. 2 (1994): 317–48; and Christine Quinn Trank, Sara L. Rynes, and Robert D. Bretz, "Attracting Applicants in the War for Talent: Differences in Work Preferences among High Achievers," *Journal of Business and Psychology* 16, no. 3 (2002): 331–45.

9. Thomas L. Webb and Paschal Sheeran, "Does Changing Behavioral Intentions Engender Behavior Change? A Meta-analysis of the Experimental Evidence," *Psychological Bulletin* 132, no.2 (2006): 249–68.

10. John P. Campbell et al., "A Theory of Performance," in *Frontiers in Industrial/Organizational Psychology: Personnel Selection and Classification,* ed. N. Schmitt and W. C. Borman (San Francisco: Jossey-Bass, 1993), 35–71.

11. Christina N. Lacerenza et al., "Leadership Training Design, Delivery, and Implementation: A Meta-analysis," *Journal of Applied Psychology* 102, no. 12 (2017): 1686–718.

12. Rebecca J. Jones, Stephen A. Woods, and Yves R.F. Guillaume, "The Effectiveness of Workplace Coaching: A Meta-analysis of Learning and Performance Outcomes from Coaching," *Journal of Occupational and Organizational Psychology* 89, no. 2 (2016): 249–77.

13. Shannon Shaper, "How Many Interviews Does It Take to Hire a Googler?," *re:Work* (blog), April 4, 2017, https://rework.withgoogle.com/blog/google-rule-of-four/.

14. Marylène Gagné and Edward L. Deci, "Self-Determination Theory and Work Motivation," *Journal of Organizational Behavior* 26, no. 4 (2005): 331–62.

15. Abraham H. Maslow, *The Farther Reaches of Human Nature* (New York: Viking Press, 1971).

16. Alan Colquitt, *Next Generation Performance Management: The Triumph of Science Over Myth and Superstition* (Charlotte, NC: Information Age Publishing Inc., 2017).

17. Christopher P. Cerasoli, Jessica M. Nicklin, and Michael T. Ford, "Intrinsic Motivation and Extrinsic Incentives Jointly Predict Performance: A 40-Year Meta-analysis," *Psychological Bulletin* 140, no. 4 (2014): 980–1008.

18. Edward L. Deci and Richard M. Ryan, "A Motivational Approach to Self: Integration in Personality," in *Perspectives on Motivation*, vol. 38 of *Nebraska Symposium on Motivation*, ed. R. Dienstbier (Lincoln: University of Nebraska Press, 1991), 237–88; and Richard M. Ryan, Edward L. Deci, and Wendy S. Grolnick, "Autonomy, Relatedness, and the Self: Their Relation to Development and Psychopathology," in *Theory and Methods*, vol. 1 of *Developmental Psychology*, ed. Dante Cicchetti and Donald J. Cohen (New York: Wiley, 1995), 618–55.

19. Frederick I. Herzberg, *Work and the Nature of Man* (Cleveland: World Publishing Company, 1966).

20. Hackman and Oldham, "Job Diagnostic Survey."

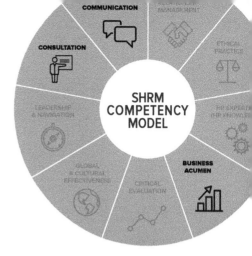

8

Communicate Your Findings

Chapter Snapshot

Questions we will answer:

- How do I communicate my findings to the stakeholders involved?
- What's the best way to present my ideas to ensure stakeholder buy-in?
- How can I present the results of analyses so they make sense and support my case?

....

Jen knows that she needs to frame her proposal in a way that wins over leadership, so she begins brainstorming with her team. They reflect on what they heard in the focus groups and interviews. The message was clear: pay was just part of the issue; there's much more to it, and many of the bigger issues can be traced to management. How can Jen explain this to managers without putting them on the defensive?

....

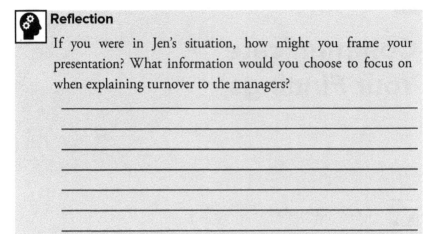

Reflection

If you were in Jen's situation, how might you frame your presentation? What information would you choose to focus on when explaining turnover to the managers?

_____

_____

_____

_____

_____

_____

When crafting a presentation, the best place to start your planning is with the audience. Knowing your audience is key to shaping your message or story. Obviously, you'll need to start by addressing exactly who the audience is, but there are several other things to take into consideration:

- What do they care about?
- What do you want them to know?
- What do you want them to do?
- How do they prefer to receive information?
- How do you want them to feel?
- What biases do they have that could make them either supportive or resistant to your message?

Once you've thought about your audience, it'll be easier to determine which data or pieces of information are most relevant. From there, you can plan accordingly.

Take a Deeper Dive

Read "Data Storytelling: Know Your Audience" by Jonathan Ferrar, founder and CEO of Ochre Rock, as well as "How to Tell a Great Story" by Carolyn O'Hara.[1]

....

Jen has gotten to know her audience pretty well since her initial communication with them. A proposal that doesn't target pay will just frustrate management. She'll need to be careful to present the findings in a way that won't turn them off from the beginning.

Jen decides to use one of the recent separations to kick off her presentation. She crafts the story: a bright, motivated employee who spent her life at the top of the class now finds herself unclear where she stands. Suddenly she's working with other people who are just as smart and motivated and she's unsure of how to stand out from the crowd. How does she progress her career now? When a recruiter calls, offering more money and playing to her ego and newfound insecurities, she feels in demand. Maybe a new company will offer more attention and new opportunities.

Now Jen has a launching point. Where does she go from there? She has to think about all of the data the team collected: focus groups, engagement surveys, performance ratings, and so on. How does she work all of that into her story?

....

Thinking of your presentation as a story gives you a clear framework for organizing your message and data. This way, you're organizing your facts into a narrative, ultimately making your case more compelling. With analytics, the goal is to change how someone behaves or makes a decision—that is, to persuade someone. You won't compel stakeholders unless they understand what you've done. When stories combine data and analytics with points of view or examples from real people, they're richer and clearer. This means your audience will be more engaged and likely more receptive.

Most good stories have a clear protagonist (a lead character). Your story should be no different. A protagonist is a great way to integrate concrete and relatable examples with your data. By describing a recent separation, Jen has centered her story around someone who will resonate with the audience.

Jen has introduced the scenario. Now how does she arrive at a solution? How can she present her data in a meaningful way? Think about any story you've read or heard. What are the defining characteristics? Each story has a setup that establishes the relevant background information, a conflict, and a resolution. Jen's presentation—and any HR analytics presentation—can be shaped the same way.

Take a Deeper Dive

Read "10 Kinds of Stories to Tell with Data" by Thomas H. Davenport.[2]

A useful exercise for outlining your presentation is storyboarding. When you storyboard, don't bother with PowerPoint or any other presentation software. Start with a blank document or even a stack of sticky notes or a whiteboard. The end goal is to create a visual outline of your presentation. Think of it like your blueprint.

To get the process started, think of your main message. What's the big idea here? If you had to communicate your findings in just a single sentence, what would you say? From there, begin jotting down all of the key points surrounding that message. Get down everything that comes to mind. You can always cut details later. Once your ideas are laid out, you can begin arranging them to flow logically.

Reflection

Given what we've uncovered in previous chapters about turnover in R&D, let's engage in some storyboarding for Jen's presentation. First, what's the big idea? In a single sentence, what's the main message she wants her audience to take away?

_____

_____

_____

_____

_____

Now list all of the key points surrounding this message. Think back to Chapter 7 when Jen sorted through all of her findings. Let your ideas flow organically here; we'll edit in the next step.

_____

_____

_____

_____

_____

_____

_____

_____

It's time to create a logical sequence. Using the boxes below, start arranging your ideas in a way that flows. Feel free to add more boxes if you need. Once you've finished, you'll have the blueprint for a presentation.

When Jen begins the storyboarding process, she realizes that she's already laid the background. She has a protagonist and she's introduced a bit about the conflict. Now, what's to blame for the protagonist leaving? While pay may be part of the story, without other contextual factors, she may not have even called the recruiter back. Now the pieces are starting to fall into place.

Jen shows the engagement data, including the key driver analysis that shows the relative importance of pay, management, and rewards and recognition to turnover intent. She uses anonymized quotations from the exit interviews, stay interviews, and focus groups. She also brings in performance data and recognition data to show that the managers' practices aren't differentiating between employees. This also shows that promotion rates are lower than the company average. Figure 8.1 shows the results of Jen's initial storyboarding.

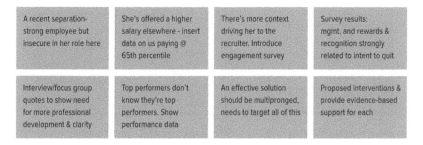

Main message: R&D employees are leaving because of an overall lack of rewards and recognition, extending well beyond salary.

A recent separation-strong employee but insecure in her role here	She's offered a higher salary elsewhere - insert data on us paying @ 65th percentile	There's more context driving her to the recruiter. Introduce engagement survey	Survey results: mgmt. and rewards & recognition strongly related to intent to quit
Interview/focus group quotes to show need for more professional development & clarity	Top performers don't know they're top performers. Show performance data	An effective solution should be multipronged, needs to target all of this	Proposed interventions & provide evidence-based support for each

Figure 8.1. Storyboarding for R&D presentation

When you're moving along in the storyboarding process, it's important to think about the final product. As you organize all of your key points, give thought again to your audience. Are your points coming across clearly to them?

The rules of horizontal and vertical logic provide a good foundation for shaping your presentation (see Figure 8.2). *Horizontal logic* refers to the headings of your presentation slides. All of your headings should read like a story. If you were to read just the heading or title of each slide, these snapshots should provide the overall story you're trying to tell. You may want to begin with an executive summary slide that lists a bullet point corresponding to each subsequent title slide. This will help you ensure your presentation flows and provides your audience with a roadmap up front for what you'll cover. *Vertical logic* happens within each slide. All information contained in a single slide should be related. The content should match the title. Any visuals should reinforce the text on the slide. No nonessential information should be included.

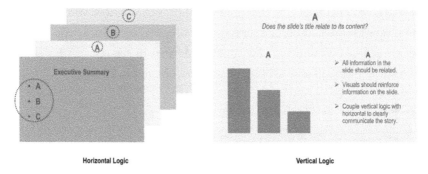

Figure 8.2. Horizontal and vertical logic in presentations

It can also be helpful to follow the *rule of three*. Essentially, you want to convey your main ideas three times: Up front, present an executive summary that lets the audience know what you're about to tell them. Then the actual content of your presentation will solidify that message. Finally, end by summarizing your message with a conclusion. Repetition helps the audience remember your message long after your presentation.

 Take a Deeper Dive

Read *TED Talks: The Official Guide to Public Speaking* by Chris Anderson.[3]

The structure and repetition of your presentation won't matter much if the data are incomprehensible. Rattling off a list of numbers won't move your audience to side with you. It may even put them to sleep! Where possible, try to present your data graphically or pictorially. Data and statistics become more accessible and easily digestible when they're presented this way. You can absorb more information faster when you're looking at a graph than when you're looking at a table or list of results.

If you've got some results you'd like to present visually, there are a few guidelines to keep in mind. First, reduce noise. As with your overall presentation, you'll want to focus on just the main ideas. This will make key relationships or patterns easy to spot. Next, determine your question before working on the visual. When you understand what you want the main idea to be, it'll be much easier to decide what kind of graph or image would be best. Table 8.1 displays some common ways of visualizing data.

Finally, be consistent. Use the same visual cues throughout your presentation. For example, if on one slide you highlight a key relationship by putting a red box around it, make sure you do that in the rest of your slides. This way your audience will know what to look for and where.

Table 8.1. Common ways of visualizing data

Type	Definition	Example Use	Image
Indicator	A headline figure allowing you to compare your data to a reference point	Has your department met its targeted annual revenue?	
Line chart	Linear display of a trend over time or across categories	How have sales increased over the past five years?	
Bar chart	Presentation of categorical data to reflect values within each category	What's the most popular recruitment source for each age group?	
Column chart	Vertical version of a bar chart, allowing for easy side-byside comparisons of different values	How many employees are leaving from each department within the company?	
Pie chart	Circular depiction of the share each category makes up of the whole	What recruitment source brings in the biggest share of total leads?	
Area chart	Line graph depicting trends over time, while also accounting for volume or proportion represented by each category	To what extent is our revenue exceeding our cost?	
Scatterplot	Set of data points plotted on x and y axes to represent two sets of variables (recall their use in correlation from Chapter 6)	How strong is the relationship between salary and employee engagement?	

Take a Deeper Dive

Read *Data Visualization Techniques* by SAS and "Visualizations That Really Work" by Scott Berinato.[4]

Reflection

Think back to the data Jen was working with in the last chapter. Table 8.2 lists some of the highlights she plans to include in her presentation. What way(s) should she visualize each?

Table 8.2. Examples of important data to include in presentation

Data Set	Major Findings	Visualization Type
Engagement scores	Scores are higher than the organization average for meaningfulness of work and regard for colleagues. Scores were lower than average for management and supervision as well as for awards and recognition.	
Performance scores	Performance ratings of separated employees are not much higher than average.	
Exit interviews	People mentioned lack of growth and development opportunities as much as low salary.	
Compensation data	Company pays at 65th percentile. R&D employees who left were more likely to be paid below the median.	

After a long and winding road, Jen is ready to present her findings and proposal to her stakeholders. In the next chapter, she'll get their reaction—and has to figure out what to do about it. Consultants and specialists often have the luxury of presenting a solution and moving on to something else. Jen doesn't have that option. As the HR director, she also has to think about implementation and evaluation. In Chapter 9, she'll tackle those topics. Luckily, analytics can help with those tasks too.

 From the SHRM Research Lab

Storytelling can be powerful because it triggers emotion. The brain processes emotions differently than facts and data. Behavioral changes are more likely to follow a story than a presentation of numbers.[5] The importance of storytelling has been observed in a number of fields. For example, the medical community has begun to practice storytelling when communicating their research findings. This has helped these findings make their way into practice.[6]

 Take a Deeper Dive

Watch "Empathy, Neurochemistry, and the Dramatic Arc" by Future of StoryTelling and pay close attention to the story of Ben.[7]

Similar to storytelling, data visualization can be an effective way of engaging your audience. To make the best use of data visualization practices, it helps to understand a bit about visual perception and cognition. These are the processes in the brain upon which design principles are based. Visual perception, or seeing, is handled by the visual cortex. This cortex is fast and efficient. We see immediately and have to expend little effort to do so. Cognition, or thinking, is handled mostly by the cerebral cortex. Compared to the visual cortex, the cerebral cortex is slower and less efficient.[8] Traditional data presentation methods, like charts and tables, require the audience to rely almost entirely on conscious thinking. However, data visualization—such as the methods listed in Table 8.1—takes advantage of our visual perception, allowing us to comprehend faster.[9]

Gestalt psychology is based on how the brain processes visual information. The main premise of Gestalt psychology is that the whole is different from the sum of its parts. From this notion a set of principles emerged to explain how the human eye and brain organize visual objects. The principles are summarized in Table 8.3.

Table 8.3. Gestalt principles

Principle	Definition	Example
Law of similarity	Objects that are similar tend to appear grouped together.	
Law of proximity	Objects that are near each other appear to be grouped together.	
Law of continuity	Lines between objects are seen as following the smoothest path rather than as multiple angles or separate pieces.	
Law of closure	Objects are grouped together if they seem to complete some entity.	
Law of good figure or simplicity	Objects are seen in a way that makes them appear as simple as possible.	

 Key Takeaways

- Any presentation of data should begin with knowing your audience. Customizing your message to the people receiving it is essential to securing their buy-in.

- Narrative storytelling is an effective framework for organizing analytics presentations. Use quantitative findings and rich, relatable examples to present a clear and compelling case.
- Support your claims by showing your audience what's going on. Consider presenting your data as a picture or graph when possible so the audience can easily see and interpret meaningful findings.

Liberty Mutual Investigates Turnover

A department with high-volume positions was experiencing elevated turnover at Liberty Mutual Insurance and sought help. Leaders turned to the talent analytics department to understand why employees were leaving and to predict future turnover rates. Although it was important to predict how many hires would be required to replace separations, the primary goal was to identify actionable drivers of turnover and take action to reduce turnover going forward.

Talent analytics gathered data from a variety of sources. They talked to stakeholders and studied exit interviews to identify key variables. Once they gathered the data, they developed turnover models to understand which variables were most predictive of voluntary turnover. One of the variables found to be associated with increased turnover was applying for positions within the company. These data were gathered from the internal ATS. The ATS is a rich data source that includes variables such as where in the company the employee applied, the outcome of the application (hired or declined), and what stage(s) of the interview process the employee completed.

A series of descriptive analyses and t-tests were performed to investigate the internal application issue. By comparing the quarterly turnover rates for those who applied for other jobs within the company and those who did not, Liberty Mutual confirmed that internal job searching was associated with an increased risk of turnover.

Further, by comparing the turnover rates of successful and unsuccessful internal applicants to other employees, Liberty Mutual discovered that unsuccessfully applying for internal positions was uniquely associated with subsequent voluntary turnover: those who applied from within and were rejected turned over at approximately twice the rate of other employees. Those rejected before receiving a phone screening were especially at risk, while employees who completed a phone screening before the rejection had turnover rates similar to employees who did not participate in any internal job searches. Additional analyses revealed that the pattern persisted for employees whose performance met or exceeded expectations.

Talent analytics developed a hypothesis that phone screening all internal applicants could provide employees with critical feedback for career development and soften the blow of rejection. Talent analytics used this information to connect with the talent acquisition and the talent management departments to better understand the rejection process as well as what could be done to improve the employee experience. A cost-benefit analysis revealed that Liberty Mutual could phone screen all internal applicants with only a modest increase in the number of full-time recruiters. Given the high cost of turnover, the additional costs associated with recruiter salary would still result in cost savings for the company.

Endnotes

1. Jonathan Ferrar, "Data Storytelling: Know Your Audience," HR Zone, October 25, 2017, https://www.hrzone.com/engage/employees/data-storytelling-know-your-audience; and Carolyn O'Hara, "How to Tell a Great Story," *Harvard Business Review*, July 30, 2014, https://hbr.org/2014/07/how-to-tell-a-great-story.
2. Thomas H. Davenport, "10 Kinds of Stories to Tell with Data," *Harvard Business Review*, May 5, 2014, https://hbr.org/2014/05/10-kinds-of-stories-to-tell-with-data.
3. Chris Anderson, *TED Talks: The Official Guide to Public Speaking* (New York: Houghton Mifflin Harcourt Publishing Company, 2016).
4. SAS, *Data Visualization Techniques: From Basics to Big Data with SAS® Visual Analytics*, white paper (Cary, NC: SAS, 2017); and Scott Berinato,

"Visualizations That Really Work," *Harvard Business Review*, June 2016, https://hbr.org/2016/06/visualizations-that-really-work.

5. Ty Bennett, *The Power of Storytelling: The Art of Influential Communication* (American Fork, UT: Sound Concepts Inc., 2013); and Buster Benson, "Cognitive Bias Cheat Sheet," *Better Humans* (blog), September 1, 2016, https://betterhumans.coach.me/cognitive-bias-cheat-sheet-55a472476b18.

6. Thomas B. Newman, "The Power of Stories over Statistics: Lessons from Neonatal Jaundice and Infant Airplane Safety," in *Narrative Research in Health and Illness*, ed. Brian Hurwitz, Trisha Greenhalgh, and Vieda Skultans (London: Wiley, 2004), 257–76.

7. Future of StoryTelling, "Empathy, Neurochemistry, and the Dramatic Arc: Paul Zak at the Future of StoryTelling 2012," October 3, 2012, Youtube, https://www.youtube.com/watch?v=q1a7tiA1Qzo.

8. Mehdi Dastani, "The Role of Visual Perception in Data Visualization," *Journal of Visual Languages and Computing* 13, no. 6 (2002): 601–22.

9. Stephen Few, *Information Dashboard Design: Displaying Data for At-a-Glance Monitoring*, 2nd ed. (Burlingame, CA: Analytics Press, 2013).

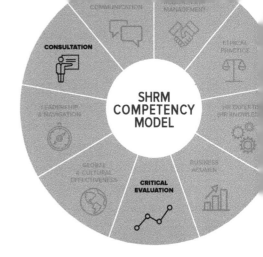

9

Evaluate Your Intervention

Chapter Snapshot

Questions we will answer:

- How can analytics help me after I implement a solution?
- What do I need to do to improve my chances of success?
- How can I evaluate the results of my project?

When we left Jen in Chapter 8, she and her team had reviewed all of their findings and assessed where evidence from the academic literature could help identify a solution and develop a plan. She had also used storytelling and visualization techniques to put all of that information into a presentation that she could share with her stakeholders.

....

Jen proposes a multifaceted approach to addressing the problem in R&D. In the short term, she suggests raising the market position of pay to the 75th percentile. She says she's working on improving the way recruitment data is captured to better track the competitiveness of the compensation package. Jen also suggests partnering with the managers to develop a plan for recognizing exemplary performance and clarifying expectations. Finally, she asks the managers how she can improve career coaching and provide more developmental opportunities. By the end of the conversation, the managers agree to a longer-term project around creating a development program. They also agree to coaching for themselves to develop their feedback and coaching skills.

....

Jen needs the R&D managers to be motivated and willing to embrace whatever changes need to be made. This requires communication and opportunities for them to provide input. Communication is key for Jen. Delivering consistent messages with a compelling case for change requires coordinated communication. Putting together a well-thought-out communication plan can help ensure you're delivering the right messages and managing your stakeholders' expectations effectively.

Take a Deeper Dive

Management of change is an important part of any initiative and can impact the timing of the effects you expect to see. Read "Change Management and Change Management Models" by RapidBi.[1]

Reflection

Who would be important stakeholders or stakeholder groups for Jen's effort? What are some ways she could reach them throughout the project?

_____

_____

_____

_____

_____

_____

_____

Jen agrees to come back in a week with an implementation plan and a way to evaluate the proposed solution over time. She makes a list of the goals her solution is trying to achieve. For each one, she then brainstorms how she'd know if the solution was effective. That process allows Jen to identify metrics and think about the change she expects to see. She then identifies where she'll get the data.

Jen puts all of the information she's written into an evaluation plan. The plan will serve as a roadmap for the analytics work throughout the implementation of her solution. She'll show her stakeholders the evaluation plan to get agreement on the expected impact and measures of success. She'll also use the plan to make sure she's captured baseline information before implementing any initiatives. This way she can evaluate the impact of the initiatives over time.

....

Take a Deeper Dive

Learn more by watching "Pretest and Posttest Analysis using Excel" by Todd Grande.[2]

....

Once Jen and the managers have agreement on the metrics, she'll determine how frequently they should be collected. She will also decide how often she'll report on the impact she sees. Jen's evaluation plan is summarized in Table 9.1.

....

Measuring the impact of the solution is critical to showing ROI. The stakeholders want to know that the money and time they invest in Jen's solution are worth it. This goes beyond time and money though. Individuals who are being asked to do something different will likely want confirmation that the energy they're investing in change is paying off. In that way, evaluating the changes can fuel momentum.

Typical methods to evaluate change initiatives are focus groups, interviews, surveys, and administrative data, such as turnover rates. An evaluative approach should begin with the goals of the initiative. What are you trying to achieve? From there, each goal should identify a way to measure progress. For example, the ultimate goal for Jen's effort was to reduce turnover in R&D. There are two metrics I've already discussed that can help her evaluate progress: turnover based on administrative records (a lagging indicator) and likelihood of leaving (i.e., turnover intent) from the engagement surveys (a leading indicator). The work that was done to redefine the problem will be a great source of the baseline metrics Jen will need to evaluate the impact of her solution.

It's important to be as comprehensive as possible in your evaluation strategy without making it too complex. If your strategy requires too much

Table 9.1. Evaluation plan for R&D solutions

Goal	Metric	Data Source	Expected Change
1. Reduce R&D turnover.	1.1. Intention to leave 1.2. R&D turnover rates	1.1. Engagement surveys 1.2. Administrative records	1.1. Decrease 1.2. Decrease
2. Improve employee satisfaction with recognition.	2.1. Average score in R&D on item	2.1. Engagement surveys	2.1 Increase
3. Improve employee satisfaction with development opportunities.	3.1. Average score in R&D on item	3.1. Engagement surveys	3.1. Increase
4. Improve employee satisfaction with management and supervision.	4.1. Average score in R&D on item	4.1. Engagement surveys	4.1. Increase
5. Improve manager self-awareness and self-efficacy.	5.1. R&D manager self-ratings	5.1. Pre-post coaching evaluation survey	5.1. Increase
6. Improve manager leadership skills, particularly feedback and coaching.	6.1. R&D employee ratings of leader behaviors	6.1. Pre-post leader 360 assessments	6.1. Increase

work, or results in findings that are hard to understand, it's unlikely the strategy will be carried out. As you develop your evaluation plan, think about how long you expect it will take to see results. Is the intervention something that should have an immediate impact? How often are you measuring that impact? What might the results look like over time? Will there be an immediate spike in results? Will that spike be maintained or temper off after a while?

Reflection

What other methods could you use to measure the extent to which the program has achieved its goals?

_____

_____

_____

Thinking about your expected results—making a hypothesis—will help you determine whether a program is having the desired result. It's possible that changes will need to be made to get the program back on course. You would never know that if you weren't evaluating it regularly. It's also important to use your hypotheses to set stakeholder expectations. Communicating the impact you expect to see will get stakeholders on the same page about the likely degree of impact and how long it will take to get there.

....

Jen goes back to the stakeholders with her implementation and evaluation plans. As she walks out of the meeting, the R&D director pulls her aside to thank her: "I know you and I got off on the wrong foot, but in the end we learned something about the department." He goes on to say that he and the managers made the same mistake they warn their employees about—forgetting to test their hypothesis.

Jen and the director shake hands. They agree that they look forward to a continued partnership throughout the implementation.

....

Reflection

How can analytics shape the way HR partners with other lines of business in the organization?

_____

_____

_____

_____

_____

The story in this book is not uncommon. In fact, multiple authors of this book have encountered something similar. HR has moved beyond the routine activities that traditionally made up personnel management, such as payroll and benefits. Now, it has a more substantive role in developing people strategies to support the organization's goals. For HR leaders to have a broader organizational impact, they too need to shift focus from HR processes to the impact of talent on the broader business strategy and outcomes.

Analytics provides a way to demonstrate that linkage. Other business functions like finance, customer service, marketing, and sales all use data extensively. This has increased the expectations and perceived importance surrounding talent-related data. The ability to bring analytics to the table enables HR professionals to be on common ground with other functions and speak a common language.

This book provides a broad introduction into what HR analytics are and how they can help you be a more effective HR partner. If you're going to be more heavily involved in analytics, this will likely be just the beginning. You'll want to continue your development in areas like statistics and research methods.

Expertise is required for good statistical analyses and analytics, but that doesn't mean you need to become a specialist. You need to know what to ask for, how to interpret it, and when something doesn't look right. If you're not interested in specializing in analytics yourself, start by finding someone in your organization who is, even if they're outside HR. You might be able to borrow capability—either from another function within your company or externally through consultants—while you build your own.

If you do want to become more proficient, start by exploring the Deeper Dive sections throughout this book. There's also a wealth of free and low-cost courses and content online, some of which we've included here. Regardless of whether you want to be an analytics pro or you just want to know enough to navigate the new data-rich reality of HR, your understanding of the business and the people in your organization are critical to making analytics work.

From the SHRM Research Lab

In this book, you saw a number of ways in which data and analytics have grown as assets to HR. This trend isn't limited to our field. Within and across organizations the data skill gap poses a problem. Many organizations are looking to citizen data scientists as a remedy. In a nutshell, this means they are investing in the employees they already have by encouraging them to get training and education in data science. This way employees can investigate their own data rather than rely on someone less intimately familiar with the data's context.

Data scientists have extensive backgrounds in computer science, coding, machine learning, and statistics. Such an extensive background takes a long time to develop and is usually highly compensated. This has posed a tremendous barrier to many organizations. But this isn't the only problem with relying solely on data experts. As organizations become more advanced, they are becoming more interested in using data to predict future outcomes. Merely relying on data from the past won't suffice. Businesses must be forward thinking in how they collect their data to best serve predictive analytics. This means the employees who collect the data (e.g., those rating performance or creating and administering an engagement survey) need to understand how those data will later be analyzed.

These conditions have created fertile ground for the growth of citizen data scientists. Employees in IT, supply chain management, marketing, HR, or any other department are now being tasked with data analytics. This doesn't mean *every* employee will become a citizen data scientist. Organizations are more inclined to choose a select few individuals who will take on data and analytics as a secondary part of their roles.

The expanding popularity of citizen data scientists is accompanied by some other emerging trends:

- **Automation.** Technology is increasingly allowing manual tasks to be automated, which allows them to be done faster and on a greater scale. Automating tasks such as data preparation will reduce the training burden on citizen data scientists.

- **Advanced and executive education.** Universities are now offering a large diversity of data science and analytics programs to meet the growing demand. While some companies may encourage employees to pursue math or social science degrees to obtain analytics training, others are looking to more basic statistics training that will allow employees to partner with a data science team.

- **Data governance.** Increasing access to organizational data increases the complexity of handling those data. As more employees become equipped to use data, the organization must have governance in place to be sure there aren't redundancies or inconsistencies in how data are being used across departments. Security also becomes a growing concern as more individuals gain access to data.

Your investment in this book might be thought of as your personal step toward becoming an HR citizen data scientist. You are probably already a domain expert. Now you're expanding your analytics repertoire to increase your ability to extract value from HR data.

 Key Takeaways

- Analytics can be useful throughout any human capital project. In addition to helping you properly redefine the problem and identify solutions, it can also help you evaluate your solutions. This enables you to identify issues early enough to improve your intervention, discontinue it if it isn't working, or demonstrate its impact to stakeholders.

- Change management is critical to any new initiative. Communication is key and can't be overdone.

- Not every HR professional needs to become an analytics specialist. However, every HR professional should understand where analytics fit into the HR landscape and how they can be harnessed.

Hilton Hotels and Resorts Focuses on Well-Being

The hospitality industry is known for high levels of turnover, which come with an astonishing cost. To combat turnover and create a great place to work for all, Hilton Hotels and Resorts continuously seeks ways to drive retention and differentiate themselves as an employer of choice in today's competitive job market. Their corporate mission is to be the most hospitable company in the world, and this mission doesn't end at the customer experience—it extends to the team-member experience as well. Hilton recognized that the well-being of team members is critical to business success and set out to identify ways to directly impact the day-to-day experiences of their team members.

Many of Hilton's innovative ideas come directly from their team members. Each year they comb through the feedback from their annual engagement survey to gain new insights. One theme that emerged highlighted opportunities to improve the spaces team members work in on-property—the areas that guests don't see, most frequently called the back of the house but renamed the "heart of the house" by Hilton. In response to this and other survey themes, Hilton introduced Thrive@Hilton, their team-member value proposition. Thrive@Hilton is an investment in the basics that seeks to evolve how those at Hilton work and make space for what matters (e.g., family, personal growth, innovation, creativity). As part of Thrive@ Hilton, Hilton committed to enhancing work environments for on-property team members. The heart-of-house initiatives are anchored around six pillars, emphasizing concepts like newly designed locker rooms, team-member restaurants and wardrobes, and improved Wi-Fi accessibility.

To measure the impact of the heart-of-house initiatives, Hilton identified key metrics to serve as success indicators. People metrics were some of the first data points that came to mind—things like turnover, satisfaction, and engagement—but they wanted to go a step further. This was an opportunity for HR to demonstrate that an investment in team members is an investment in the business.

Including success indicators that are major business metrics, such as revenue, help to tell a comprehensive story. To facilitate this, Hilton tracked people and business success indicators pre- and post-intervention for each hotel that made the heart-of-house commitment.

What started as a small pilot has now impacted thousands of team members around the world. Even though Hilton is still early on in their global rollout, the positive impacts of these investments are already visible in the success indicators previously defined. Hilton's HR team began to pull together a simple and concise story, supporting statements with digestible data points, to provide an update to senior leaders and owners. The heart-of-house journey was summarized, from initial metrics, to program implementation, to survey feedback. The final story they produced ultimately connected HR to the business, highlighting that in general, hotels with completed heart-of-house enhancements were experiencing reductions in turnover, improved engagement and pride, and even increases in hotel revenue and customer satisfaction.

Endnotes

1. RapidBi Support, "Change Management and Change Management Models," RapidBi, May 10, 2016, https://rapidbi.com/changemanagement/.
2. Todd Grande, "Pretest and Posttest Analysis Using Excel," Youtube, December 2, 2014, https://www.youtube.com/watch?v=LZxaMmCZFm4.

A

How Analytics Fit into the SHRM Competency Model

Purpose

The appetite for and impact of analytics continues to grow exponentially in today's technology era. You'll need the right people and skills in place to build your organization's analytical function to withstand changes and remain relevant to the business. This section highlights how HR analytics fit into *The SHRM Body of Competency and Knowledge* (SHRM BoCK, see figure A.1)—which defines the competencies and knowledge necessary for effective practice as an HR professional and serves as the basis for the SHRM-CP and SHRM-SCP certification exams—and what it means for you as you develop your analytics capabilities.[1]

In HR, analytics involves using human resources data (e.g., attendance records, promotion rates, engagements scores) and business analytics techniques to produce metrics that report company performance (e.g., business outcomes) relative to goals. People drive business outcomes, meaning the analytics that help organizations understand the people behind their operations are an extremely valuable tool. Further, HR can use insights gleaned through analytics to predict future business outcomes and optimize employee performance. Instead of relying on intuition-based recommendations, analytics enable HR to make data-driven decisions and deliver quantitative and more objective forecasts and recommendations. HR professionals must be proficient in critical evaluation to do this effectively.

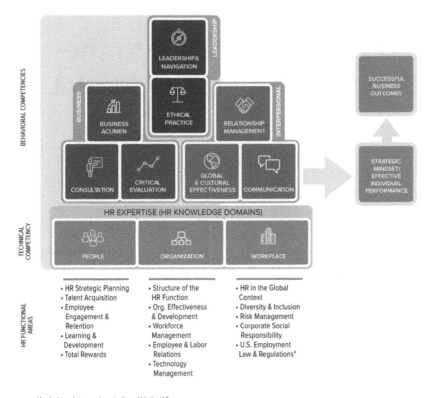

Figure A.1. SHRM Body of Competency and Knowledge (SHRM BoCK)

Identify the Competencies

SHRM BoCK defines *critical evaluation* as "the knowledge, skills, abilities, and other characteristics (KSAOs) needed to collect and analyze qualitative and quantitative data, and to interpret and promote findings that evaluate HR initiatives and inform business decisions and recommendations." [2] It is one of nine competencies that describe what it takes to be a successful HR professional and a critical business partner in the organization.

Four subcompetencies compose critical evaluation: data advocacy, data gathering, data analysis, and evidence-based decision-making. In addition, an HR professional proficient in critical evaluation possesses the following foundation elements:

- Survey and assessment tools
- Sources of data

- Basic concepts in statistics and measurement
- Ability to interpret data and charts
- Talent for building evidence-based strategies

People often use *Critical Evaluation* to help them identify a potential problem. Following root-cause identification, you can use data analysis to help identify potential solutions, select the best solution, implement an initiative, and evaluate its effectiveness. Analysis of available data drives each step of this frequently cyclical process. However, the HR competencies do not exist in isolation of each other. Rather, they work together and complement each other. HR expertise (the technical competency in SHRM BoCK) serves as the foundational knowledge for HR practice. Behavioral competencies—like critical evaluation, business acumen, communication, leadership and navigation, relationship management, global and cultural effectiveness, consultation, and ethical practice—are what enable practitioners to apply HR knowledge to solve organizational challenges effectively.

For example, effective HR professionals not only understand the organization's operations and functions, but are also in tune with what is taking place in the external environment. In other words, effective HR professionals are proficient in business acumen, but to tailor recommendations to their organization's specific industry, size, sector, geographical location, and so on, they must also employ critical evaluation and HR expertise.

Competencies Applied to This Story

Recall that in Chapter 1, Jen used data and metrics like turnover rates to help her investigate the concerns of the R&D managers. First, she looked at overall turnover for R&D compared to the overall turnover for the organization. She recognized that the turnover rates were average for the manufacturing industry and for R&D employees. Her understanding of the external environment demonstrated her business acumen. Of course, she learned that there was more to that story, so her critical evaluation came into play to unveil what else was going on.

As the R&D managers (and other organizational stakeholders) continued to express concern for employee separations, Jen applied her critical thinking to identify other available data sources. She then assessed the accuracy and validity of her data sets. All the data Jen collected enabled her to determine the factors contributing to R&D employees' turnover intent, or likelihood to leave the organization. But there were other competencies Jen employed in solving this business challenge.

She leveraged her proficiency in relationship management when working with her team to collect data, and throughout her interactions with stakeholders. Jen frequently communicated with stakeholders and provided status updates throughout the story, which required demonstrating her communication proficiency. Communication was also key when she had to recommend additional data collection (the employee focus groups and interviews with R&D managers) and justify the rationale for that additional resource investment. Finally, Jen's consultation proficiency came into play when it was time to report her finding that pay was not the number-one reason for separations.

After evaluating the challenges within the R&D workforce, Jen based her recommended solution on data and analyses. Then she coached the R&D management team and explained that the best intervention was manager training—not increased pay.

All of Jen's HR competencies were used at some point in her story. With business needs constantly changing based on factors such as growth and maturity level of the company, the HR profession must remain agile and adaptable. To ensure that HR professionals continue to be strategic business partners in the company, HR competencies must be the focus of continual learning and development.

Endnotes

1. Society for Human Resource Management. *The SHRM Body of Competency and Knowledge* (Alexandria: Society for Human Resource Management, 2017), https://www.shrm.org/certification/Documents/SHRM-BoCK-FINAL.pdf.
2. Society for Human Resource Management, *SHRM Body of Competency*, 30.

B

Assess Yourself

Purpose

In Chapter 2, we talked about how, in order to be good at HR analytics, you need an understanding of three domains: people, business, and data. Where do you stand on each? The purpose of this appendix is to help you identify where you can leverage the strengths you already have and where you might want to invest more of your development time. While a majority of this content is covered throughout the book chapters, some topics might sound a bit unfamiliar, but don't fret! This was done to help you identify your growth edge, even if you've mastered most of the content in this book.

Instructions

Follow the steps below to assess yourself on the people, business, and data domains. In Step 1, you'll assess your confidence. In Step 2, you'll assess your knowledge in the data domain. In Step 3, you'll evaluate your results, reflect on where you are today, and think about how to further develop.

Step 1. Assess your confidence.

Rate your level of confidence with each of the following items. Select one rating per item.

Item	Statement	Not at all Confident (1)	Somewhat Confident (2)	Very Confident (3)
1	My organization captures the data I need to address key people questions.			
2	I understand the role specific jobs and people processes in my company play in creating its competitive advantage.			
3	I can look at output and know if something doesn't look right.			
4	I can identify the top three issues business leaders in my company care about.			
5	I am comfortable with the quality of the people data in my organization.			
6	I can see where our company's culture enhances and where it impedes executing the strategy.			
7	I understand what makes our employees committed and willing to put in extra effort.			
8	I can articulate my company's competitive advantage.			
9	I know how the business works both financially and operationally.			
10	I understand how to improve the performance of a team.			
11	I can use data to inform most of the important decisions my organization must make.			
12	I can identify the drivers of effective performance and execution of my company's strategy.			
13	I am fluent with the terminology of finance, sales, marketing, and operations.			

Item	Statement	Not at all Confident (1)	Somewhat Confident (2)	Very Confident (3)
14	I understand how to enlist the support of others on change initiatives.			
15	I know what analyses are needed to address a business question.			

Step 2. Dive deeper into data.

Select the best answer for each of the following questions.

1. A company wanted to determine the healthcare cost of its employees. A sample of twenty-five employees were interviewed and their medical expenses for the previous year were determined. Later the company discovered the highest medical expense in the sample was mistakenly recorded as ten times the actual amount. However, after correcting the error, the corrected amount was still greater than or equal to any other medical expense in the sample. Which of the following sample statistics must have remained the same after the correction was made?

    a. Mean
    b. Median
    c. Mode
    d. Range
    e. Variance

6. An employee resource group wants to conduct an inclusion survey. It wants to begin with a simple random sample of sixty employees. Which of the following survey methods will produce a simple random sample?

    a. Survey the first sixty employees to arrive at work in the morning.
    b. Survey every tenth employee entering the cafeteria until sixty employees are surveyed.

    c. Use random numbers to choose fifteen employees each from four departments.

    d. Number the cafeteria seats. Use a table of random numbers to choose seats and interview the employee until sixty have been interviewed.

    e. Number the employees in the HRIS system. Assign random numbers to choose sixty employees from the employee roster for the survey.

3. Your annual engagement survey has consistently shown that your managers and employees are dissatisfied with the performance appraisal system. In particular, it is perceived as unfair, as demonstrated by the average score for that survey item. You implement a new performance appraisal system and want to compare the average fairness score in the survey administration prior to the implementation to the average fairness score after the administration. You realize that your data violate the assumption of normality. Which of the following tests could you use to evaluate where fairness perceptions improved after the new system was implemented?

    a. Paired-samples t-test

    b. Mann-Whitney

    c. Chi square

    d. MANOVA

4. A bubble chart is best used for which of the following?

    a. Change in value of a consistent metric over time.

    b. The distribution of data around a single value.

    c. How a subset of data compares to the larger whole.

    d. How two or more values compare to each other in relative magnitude.

5. The primary goal of principal component analysis is to:

    a. Divide a set of multivariate observations into classes.

    b. Assign a particular multivariate observation to one of several classes.

    c. Characterize the correlation structure between two sets of variables by replacing them with two smaller sets of variables that are highly correlated.

    d. Find the variables among a set of predictor variables that are the best predictors of a set of variables of interest.

    e. Explain the variability in a large set of variables by replacing it with a smaller set of transformed variables that explains a large portion of the total variability.

6. Which of the following is typically the *first* step in data cleaning?

    a. Examine frequency distributions.

    b. Standardize your variables.

    c. Test statistical assumptions.

    d. Impute missing values.

7. Data mapping is a critical step in which of the following data processes?

    a. Cleaning

    b. Transformation

    c. Extraction

    d. Visualization

8. In SQL programming language, you can use the conditional expression "ORDER BY" to do which of the following?

    a. Create records.

    b. Find records.

    c. Rearrange records.

    d. Select records.

9. You are working with an employee data set and identify those cases without an employee ID in the record. This is an example of which of the following validation checks?

    a. Logic check

    b. Hash total

    c. Uniqueness check

    d. Presence check

    e. Range check

10. As part of a workforce-planning initiative, you want to predict whether the employees in a particular program will stay or leave the organization. You use archival data—attendance, performance ratings, and tenure—to predict that outcome. Which of the following analytic methods could you use?
    a. Discriminant analysis
    b. Bivariate regression
    c. Two-factor ANOVA
    d. Effect size

Step 3. Reflect on your results.

It's time to reflect on where you are today. First, reflect on your confidence level. Add your scores from Step 1 in each of the three domains—people, business, and data. To calculate your score, first award 1 point for every answer marked "Not at all confident," 2 points for answers marked "Somewhat confident," and 3 points for answers marked "Very confident." Then total the points across the item numbers as indicated. Once you have your score for each domain, you can assign rank. The highest rank (1) should indicate your strongest domain.

Domain	Item Numbers	Score (5–15)	Rank (1–3)
People	2, 6, 7, 10, 14		
Business	4, 8, 9 ,12, 13		
Data	1, 3, 5, 11, 15		

Which domain is your strength? How can you lean on that strength to help you in your analytics journey?

_____

_____

_____

In which domain are you least confident? What steps might you take to learn more?

_____

_____

_____

Now that you've identified where you're most confident, it's time to assess your data- domain knowledge. If you're like many HR professionals, you might feel less confident about your skills in the data domain. Sometimes you don't know what you don't know. Score your answers on the items in Step 2 to help you focus your future development.

Answer Key

1. B	5. E	9. D
2. E	6. A	10. A
3. B	7. B	
4. D	8. C	

How did you do? If you got seven or more questions right, you may be ready for more advanced analytics! If not, don't worry—data is a big, broad domain. These items covered a range of data topics including extraction, cleaning, transformation, management, analysis, data visualization, and validation.

Which concepts were the least familiar?

_____

_____

_____

Think about which areas you might want to explore more. What commitments do you want to make to yourself to continue your data domain development?

_____

_____

_____

Many of the "Deeper Dive" resources throughout this book provide great places to start. If you'd like to test your knowledge with more items, consider this additional resource: Dishashree Gupta, "41 Questions on Statistics for Data Scientists and Analysts," *Analytics Vidhya* (blog), May 4, 2017, www.analyticsvidhya.com/blog/2017/05/41-questions-on-statisitics-data-scientists-analysts/.

C

Evaluate Your Data

Purpose

Throughout the book, Jen and her team had to spend time identifying data sources to address their challenge. They also continued to uncover challenges and concerns with the data they had available. Use this appendix to identify the data you have available to address the business challenge you're facing. This appendix will also help you evaluate the quality of the data you have on hand.

Instructions

Follow the instructions in each of the six steps below to evaluate your data. In each step, you'll find some tips to help you along the way.

Step 1. Identify the business challenges.

1a. Make a list of the top five to ten business challenges your company is facing.

If you're not sure, consider how you might be able to learn more about the business:

- Have you reviewed your company's strategic plan or those of different business units recently?
- Does your organization have an internal social media account?
- Can you arrange coffee chats or interviews with key business and organizational leaders?

- What can you learn from data you already collect, such as engagement survey results, turnover, or information from HRBPs and employee relations?

_____

_____

_____

_____

_____

_____

1b. Select the challenge you will address.

This step will be easy if you are being asked to step in and solve a pressing problem. If not, prioritize the list you made in Step 1a. Challenges that are most closely aligned with your company's competitive advantage (how you make money or fulfill your mission) are prime targets because any solution will be highly valued. Another factor to consider is whether the following conditions for successful change are being met:

- Committed leadership
- Need for change
- Powerful vision
- Critical mass
- Resources for effective implementation

Potential to modify people practices to support the change (e.g., if you can't afford to pay more, it may not make sense to select a problem that is closely linked to salaries being too low)

In evaluating challenges, identify whether the challenge has come up in the past. If so, what has been tried before? What worked or didn't work about that solution? If the challenge has come up before and a solution was not identified, why not?

_____

_____

_____

Step 2. Identify the people side of the business challenge.

What people and processes support the business challenge? Consider the following aspects:

- Culture, norms, compensation, rewards, recognition
- Leadership and management
- Individual knowledge, skills, abilities, and other characteristics
- Attitudes and motivation

_____

_____

_____

Step 3. Write a challenge/problem statement.

Write a short description of the problem. The statement should be succinct but address the five Ws:

- **Who** does the problem affect?
- **What** is the issue?
- **When** does the issue occur or when does it need to be fixed?
- **Where** is the issue occurring?
- **Why** is it important that we fix the problem (i.e., what's the business impact)?

As an example, in Jen's story, the challenge statement could be written as follows: "R&D managers are complaining that turnover has become an issue over the past year. They are losing some of their best employees and no longer have the bandwidth to complete necessary projects, putting their department goals at risk."

_____

_____

_____

Step 4. Identify the relevant data you have access to.

Think broadly about the data sources you have access to. What do you have in your HRIS system, learning and development platform, or ATS?

What data are the business units routinely collecting (e.g., customer relationship management [CRM] data)? What subscriptions do you have or could you gain access to that might provide a source for external benchmarking (e.g., from professional or trade associations)?

As you review the data you have at your disposal, think about the pros and cons of each data source. No data are perfect, but make sure you consider the following factors:

- Trustworthiness
  - Are the data complete?
  - Are they accurate?
  - Are quality control or validation procedures in place?
- Usability
  - Can you get access to the data?
  - What timeframe do the data cover? How recently or frequently are they collected?
- Reliability and standardization
  - Is there an agreed upon definition?
  - Do the data exist in multiple systems? Are they comparable?
- Are processes in place to ensure consistency?

Use the next table to help walk you through this process.

Data Source	Relevant Data/Metric	Evaluation
Employee Survey Data		Pros: Cons:
Performance, Productivity, or Efficiency Data		Pros: Cons:

Data Source	Relevant Data/Metric	Evaluation
Demographic Data		Pros: Cons:
Learning and Development Data		Pros: Cons:
Recruitment and Selection Data		Pros: Cons:
Compensation Data		Pros: Cons:
Attendance Data		Pros: Cons:
Recognition (e.g., awards, bonuses, promotion) Data		Pros: Cons:
Attendance Data		Pros: Cons:
Operational or Financial Data		Pros: Cons:
Other		Pros: Cons:

Step 5. Put the data in context.

In Chapter 2, you saw how evaluating data in context can make a big impact on the conclusions you draw. There are two broad ways to help contextualize your data:

- **Internal benchmarking.** Consider where you might be able to gather information to put the data and metrics in a broader context within your organization. Can you compare one department to another? Do you have data over time that allow you to compare information from the same quarter, for example, across years?
- **External benchmarking.** Looking outside the organization can help you gain awareness of macro trends that might be impacting your organization and provide some insight into what "high," "low," and "average" look like in a broader sense. All organizations are different, so be cautious not to rely too heavily on external benchmarks. You can gain access to external benchmarking data through professional or trade associations, or specialized vendors.

_____

_____

_____

Step 6. Identify the data you wish you had.

Review your responses to Steps 4 and 5. Where are there holes in content or quality? How might you collect new data to fill in those holes? The following are a few examples of how you might collect new data: interviews or focus groups, surveys, and new administrative data collection (e.g., adding a new variable to the employment application).

As you consider collecting new data, evaluate the feasibility. How resource intensive would it be to collect the data? You might be willing to collect data even if it will be difficult, so long as the data will be valuable in addressing the challenge.

Gap or Question	Possible Source	Feasibility

D

Choose Your HR Metrics

Purpose

In Chapter 9, Jen committed to ongoing evaluation of the initiatives she proposed. Basic metrics and reports can be relatively simple and quick solutions to keeping others informed. The purpose of this appendix is to provide you with resources that will help you choose metrics relevant to the challenge you identified in Appendix C and plan how you might track and report them over time.

Instructions

Follow the steps below to choose your metrics and develop a plan to report them. In Step 1, you'll select metrics relevant to the problem statement you identified in Appendix C. In Step 2, you'll determine how to track the metrics and communicate them to your stakeholders. In Step 3, you will create a production schedule to help track the reports you produce regularly.

Step 1. Choose your metrics.

Table D.1 indicates the broader HR categories used to organize metrics. Table D.2, the HR metrics glossary, lists specific metrics that align to each of the broader categories. It also defines the metric and describes how to compute it. Review the HR metrics glossary below to identify metrics relevant to the problem statement you created in Step 3 of Appendix C. Note that, in some cases, there may be more than one way to calculate the metric. It is important to make sure you know how it is computed in your organization and that it is consistent across data owners and stakeholders. Refer to SHRM's website for a more extensive list of HR metrics.[1]

Table D.1. HR metrics categories

Compensation	Retention
HR Function Efficiency	Talent Acquisition
Learning and Development (L&D)	Well-Being
Productivity	Workforce Demographics

Table D.2. HR metrics glossary

Metric Name	Definition	Calculation
Compensation		
Labor Cost per Full-Time Equivalent (FTE)	Company's labor cost spread evenly across FTEs	Total company labor cost ÷ total FTE count
Benefits as a Percentage of Labor Costs	Total benefits costs as a percentage of total labor costs	Total benefits cost ÷ total company labor costs
Compa-ratio	Reports the percent difference between actual salary and salary midpoint of the pay range	Employee's annual FTE salary ÷ midpoint of the salary pay range
HR Function Efficiency		
HR Cost per FTE	Total HR cost spread evenly across total FTEs count	Total HR costs ÷ total FTE count
HR Expense Percent	Percent of operating cost attributed to HR expenses	Total HR costs ÷ total operating cost
HR FTE Ratio	Number of FTEs per one HR FTE (useful to assess size of HR staff)	Total Company FTE count ÷ total HR FTE count
L&D		
L&D Investment per FTE	Dollars invested in L&D spread evenly across FTEs	Total L&D cost ÷ total FTE count

Metric Name	Definition	Calculation
L&D Hours per FTE	Total hours spent on L&D spread evenly across FTEs	Total L&D hours ÷ total FTE count
L&D FTE Ratio	Total FTE for each L&D FTE	Total FTE count ÷ total L&D FTE count
Productivity		
Revenue per FTE	Total revenue spread evenly across FTEs	Total company revenue ÷ total FTE count
Human Capital ROI	Rate of return for total investment in employees	{[Revenue − (operating cost − labor cost)] ÷ labor cost} − 1
Absenteeism Rate	Total work days missed due to illness per FTE	Total sick days used ÷ total FTE count
Retention		
Cost of Voluntary Turnover	Average cost to replace an employee who left voluntarily (i.e., resignation or retirement).	Total employees' projected base salary cost ÷ total voluntary separations of employees
Turnover Rate	Percent of workforce that left the company in a given time period	Voluntary separations + involuntary terminations ÷ average headcount
First Year Turnover Rate	Percent of workforce with a tenure of one year or less who resign (formula applicable to any tenure groups)	Resignations with a tenure of one year or less ÷ average headcount of employees with a tenure of one year or less
Talent Acquisition		
Cost per External Hire	Average recruitment costs spread evenly across external hires.	Costs associated with recruiting ÷ external recruits
External Time to Fill	Average number of calendar days to fill a position externally.	Days to fill ÷ external recruits
External Hire Rate	Employees hired externally as a percentage of headcount.	External hires ÷ total employee headcount
Well-Being		
Cost of Workers' Compensation Claims	Total claim costs spread evenly across all employees	Total claims cost ÷ total employee Headcount

(continued)

Metric Name	Definition	Calculation
Percent of Sick Days Taken	Percent of sick days used out of total sick days offered	(Total sick days taken ÷ total sick days offered) × 100
Workplace Accident Rates	Percentage of accidents per employee during a period of time (within the specific operational area)	Number of accidents in an operational area in a period of time ÷ total hours worked in the same operational area
Workforce Demographics		
Promotion Rate	Employees promoted as a percentage of total headcount	Employee promotions ÷ total employee headcount
Churnover	Rate of internal movement by employees as a percentage of total headcount	(Promotions + demotions + transfers) ÷ total employee headcount
Diversity Percentage	Employees protected by EEO law as a percentage of the total headcount	Protected class employees ÷ total employee headcount

Step 2. Communicate with stakeholders.

Frequent communication with stakeholders helps ensure buy-in, demonstrate impact, and stimulate continuous input and alignment. Metrics can be a powerful tool to track progress and communicate with stakeholders on an ongoing basis. Once you've selected your metrics in Step 1, it's a good idea to ensure that your stakeholders agree to those metrics and to establish the frequency with which you'll review them. If you're going to be tracking the metrics regularly, think about creating a report or dashboard. It can be as simple as a spreadsheet or it can involve specialized software. Think about how you want to communicate your metrics and consider the following questions:

- Who needs access to the metrics?
- How often will they be updated? Will they track data in real time, be updated at set intervals, or updated as needed or ad hoc?

- Will they be accompanied by a visualization?

_____

_____

_____

Step 3. Establish a reporting schedule.

In Step 2, you considered the frequency of your reports. The frequency should align to the fluctuation of your data. If your metrics don't change often, you won't need to produce reports often either. Think about how quickly the data can be acted upon, when the data are available, and how often they change. As you begin to use analytics more regularly, you are likely to find that you will have multiple reports that you are expected to produce regularly (e.g., a quarterly HR dashboard). At that point, it can be helpful to create a production report schedule. A production report schedule provides a tool to track the HR metrics reports created by you or your team. The schedule can help manage your time and workload, and assess what information is useful, missing, or redundant across reports. The template below offers several factors you can use to capture important reporting aspects when creating a schedule.

Production Report Schedule				
Cadence	Report	Audience	Dissemination Method	Purpose
Quarterly (first of quarter)	HR Dashboard	Senior Leadership Team (SLT)	Post to SharePoint site	Update SLT on key performance indicators (KPIs) using HR metrics

Endnote

1. Society for Human Resource Management, "Metrics List," Excel document, accessed February 9, 2018, https://www.shrm.org/ResourcesAndTools/business-solutions/Documents/Metrics-List.xlsx.

Identify Your Stakeholders

Purpose

In Chapter 2, Jen walked into a room and found many of her stakeholders staring back at her. That awkward meeting might have been avoided if she had thought more carefully about who was invested in R&D's business problem at the outset. This appendix will help you conduct a stakeholder analysis before starting your project. You can also use it to reassess the analysis throughout the project.

The purpose of a stakeholder analysis is to identify individuals and groups that can impact or are impacted by the outcomes of the project. Identifying these stakeholders early can help you define the project, assess its potential impact, and create a compelling story tailored to each audience. The exercise below will help identify project stakeholders, their level of importance to the project, and offer insight to use while developing the communication plan.

Instructions

Follow Steps 1 and 2 below to identify and prioritize your stakeholders. In Step 3, you can use the matrix provided to develop an engagement plan.

Step 1. Identify potential stakeholders.

Hold a brainstorming session with your project team to discuss which individuals or groups might be stakeholders. If available, use a whiteboard or flipchart to facilitate idea generation during the session. Use the questions below to help guide the conversation.

- Who will be directly involved in the project?
- Who might be indirectly involved in the project?
- Who might be financially or emotionally invested in the project or its outcomes?
- Who will be the gatekeepers of the project's resources?
- Who has the authority to impact the project process or outcomes?
- What are some of the outcomes we expect?
- Which individuals or groups might be positively impacted by the outcomes? What about negatively?

_____

_____

_____

_____

_____

Step 2. Assess the stakeholder's level of interest.

You probably have a substantial list of potential stakeholders. It's time to prioritize those and determine who has the most incurred risk. One common and simple approach is to create an influence-interest grid like the one in Figure E.1.

The influence-interest grid is a way to prioritize and organize stakeholders. This grid will also be useful when you begin to develop your communication plan (see Appendix L). The two basic questions below will help you assign each stakeholder to a specific quadrant on the grid.

- From low to high, what is the stakeholder's level of influence on the project and its outcomes?
  - o Low influence group: bottom two quadrants
  - o High influence group: top two quadrants

- From low to high, what is the stakeholder's level of interest in the project or its outcomes?
  - ○ Low interest group: left two quadrants
  - ○ High interest group: right two quadrants

In the section below you will see two additional grids. The first (Figure E.2) is an example of a completed grid based on the stakeholders from Jen's story. The final grid (Figure E.3) is your grid to use when completing your own stakeholder analysis.

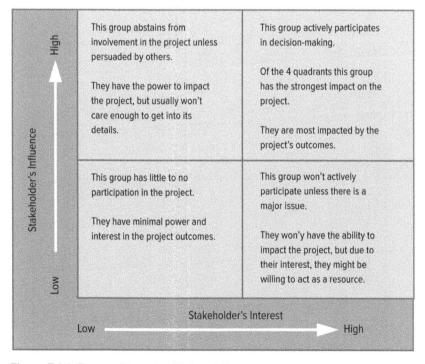

Figure E.1. Influence-Interest grid description

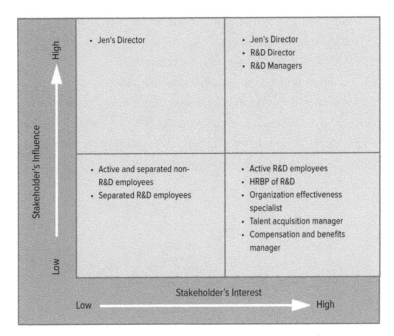

Figure E.2. Jen's Influence-Interest grid

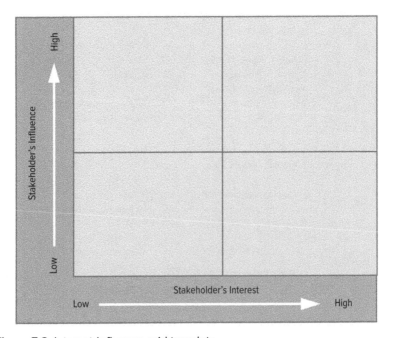

Figure E.3. Interest-Influence grid template

Step 3. Analyze stakeholder role.

Now that you've prioritized your stakeholders, complete the matrix to identify each stakeholder's role, what each cares most about, and your strategy for engaging with them.

Stakeholder Name	Contact Information	What does the stakeholder care about?	How can the stakeholder contribute to the project?	How can the stakeholder impede the project?	What strategy will engage the stakeholder?

Develop Your Hypotheses

Purpose

In Chapter 5, we talked about the importance of formulating multiple alternative hypotheses in addition to your initial hypothesis. This step can help you identify the analyses you will want to run to test those hypotheses. It will also ensure that you have or are collecting all the variables necessary to run your analyses.

Instructions

Complete the four steps in this appendix to (1) write your hypotheses, (2) list the variables you will need to test each hypothesis, (3) identify the sources of the data for each variable, and (4) record descriptive statistics for each variable.

Step 1. Write your hypotheses.

Recall from Chapter 4 that a hypothesis is a prediction about what will happen, written as an if-then statement: "If _____[I do this]_____, then _____[this]_____ will happen." Here are a few more tips to help you construct your hypotheses:

- Use clear and simple language.
- Keep your variables in mind to ensure they are easy to measure (e.g., if you've identified "turnover" as a metric, use that language in the hypothesis too).
- Make it testable. This means it needs to be specific.

Hypothesis A

_____

_____

_____

Hypothesis B

_____

_____

_____

Hypothesis C

_____

_____

_____

Hypothesis D

_____

_____

_____

Hypothesis E

_____

_____

_____

Step 2. List the variables you will need.

List the variables you will need to test each hypothesis. In Chapter 4, we defined variables simply as anything that can be measured or counted, such as turnover, salary, or engagement. Examples of variables you may need are listed below:

- Salary
- Time to fill
- Cost per hire
- Turnover

- Headcount
- Absences
- Attrition
- Employee age, gender, languages spoken
- Satisfaction
- Commitment
- Engagement
- Performance
- Motivation

Step 3. Identify your data sources.

Jen and her team came up with a list of data sources that might help them test their hypotheses. Now it's your turn. Link the variables you identified in Step 2 to each of your hypotheses from Step 1. Then use the table below to identify a data source. Don't worry if your company isn't currently collecting the necessary data. This activity can be a great way to identify areas where you might want to start collecting data. Consider the following examples of data sources:

- Surveys (exit, recruitment, engagement, satisfaction, etc.)
- Focus groups with employees or leadership
- Interviews with employees or leadership
- Financial statements
- Performance management system
- External benchmarks
- Payroll system
- Learning management system
- Workforce management system

Use the next table to help organize your potential sources of data.

Hypothesis	Variables needed to test hypothesis	Data source	New data collection or existing data?
A	1.	1.	1.
	2.	2.	2.
	3.	3.	3.
	4.	4.	4.
B	1.	1.	1.
	2.	2.	2.
	3.	3.	3.
	4.	4.	4.
C	1.	1.	1.
	2.	2.	2.
	3.	3.	3.
	4.	4.	4.
D	1.	1.	1.
	2.	2.	2.
	3.	3.	3.
	4.	4.	4.

(continued)

Hypothesis	Variables needed to test hypothesis	Data source	New data collection or existing data?
E	1.	1.	1.
	2.	2.	2.
	3.	3.	3.
	4.	4.	4.

Step 4. Record descriptive statistics for each variable.

In Chapter 5, Jen ran some basic analyses on her data to describe it. Use the table below to record some descriptive information about your data. Refer back to Chapter 5 for more information about each of the columns in the table.

Hypothesis	Variables needed to test hypothesis	n	Count or frequency	Average* or percent	SD	Minimum	Maximum
A	1.						
	2.						
	3.						
	4.						

(continued)

Hypothesis	Variables needed to test hypothesis	n	Count or frequency	Average* or percent	SD	Minimum	Maximum
B	1.						
	2.						
	3.						
	4.						
C	1.						
	2.						
	3.						
	4.						
D	1.						
	2.						
	3.						
	4.						
E	1.						
	2.						
	3.						
	4.						

* While the average is the mean, it can be substituted with the median if that's a better indicator for your data. Refer to Chapter 5 for when to use each measure of central tendency.

G

Choose Your Statistical Test

Purpose

Throughout the story, Jen and her analyst used different statistical analyses depending on the question they were trying to answer at the time. In Appendix F, you identified your hypotheses. The purpose of this appendix is to identify the statistical test you'll need to test each of those hypotheses. One of our objectives when writing this book was to provide you with enough information to get started with analytics and provide options of where to go next. For that reason, you may not recognize some of the terms and analyses mentioned in this appendix. But have no fear! At the end of this appendix you'll find additional resources and references to online interactive decision trees in case you need some additional support or prefer other formats.

Instructions

Start by answering some basic questions about the data that you have or the data that you plan to collect (e.g., What type of data do you have?) in Step 1. In Step 2, the decision tree will provide some general guidance for which analysis or analyses you could run. Please keep in mind that the analysis recommendations are broad guidelines. In many cases, data can be analyzed in multiple ways depending on factors such as your research questions, the expected outcome, the variable types, sample size, and the goal of your analysis. I understand that everyone starts with a slightly different knowledge base. If you come across a term that you don't recognize, reference the additional resources for a glossary of statistical terms.

Step 1. Identify your variable types.

In Appendix F, you made a list of each of your variables. Before selecting your analysis, you'll need to determine whether each variable is a predictor or criterion, and what type of data you have. Refer to Chapter 4 for definitions.

Variable	Variable Type (predictor or criterion)	Data Type (nominal, ordinal, interval, ratio)

Step 2. Determine what you want to do with your data.

Different statistical tests are used to make different kinds of inferences. For each of your hypotheses, determine what you want to do with your data—describe, compare, explain, or predict. For example, if you want to know whether the average engagement scores differ between two departments, you might want to use your data to compare average engagement scores between the two departments. Use the table below to determine what you want to do with your data for each of your hypotheses.

Hypothesis	Function (Describe, Compare, Explain, Predict)
A.	
B.	
C.	
D.	
E.	

Step 3. Choose your statistical test.

For each hypothesis, use the decision tree in Figure G.1 to determine which analysis to run. The boxes that aren't tinted indicate analyses you could choose. Record your planned analysis in the table below.

Hypothesis	Statistical Test
A.	
B.	
C.	
D.	
E.	

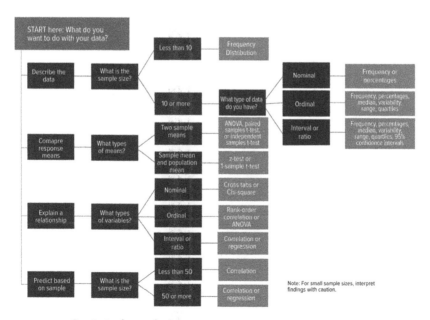

Figure G.1. Statistical test decision tree

Additional Resources

A few of the analyses mentioned in this appendix were not covered in the book (e.g., Chi square, z-test, and various t-tests). If you are a looking to learn more, here are some additional resources to get you started.

- David Lane, *HyperStat Online: An Introductory Statistics Textbook,* last modified March 1, 2008, http://davidmlane.com/hyperstat/index.html. Topics covered include normal distribution, sampling distribution, confidence intervals, Analysis of Variance (ANOVA) tests, Chi square tests, effect size, and more.
- Shawna Jackson et al., "Statistics: An Introduction," Colorado State University, 2012, https://writing.colostate.edu/guides/guide.cfm?guideid=67. A high-level overview of descriptive versus inferential statistics and an introduction to the different types of analyses used to measure each (e.g., measures of variation, t-tests, correlation, regression).
- Statsoft, "Statistics Glossary," accessed February 9, 2018, http://www.statsoft.com/Textbook/Statistics-Glossary. A glossary of statistical terms.

Additional Decision Trees

This appendix has one example of how to determine which statistical analysis you should use. There are other decision trees available to you that go into more depth or are interactive. Explore these tools to learn more.

- Charlie Kufs, "The Right Tool for the Job," *Stats with Cats Blog,* August 27, 2010, www.statswithcats.wordpress.com/2010/08/27/the-right-tool-for-the-job/. A flow chart with five different decision points.
- Office of Planning, Assessment, Research and Quality, "Quantitative Data Analysis: Choosing a Statistical Test," University of Wisconsin-Stout, December 4, 2015, http://wwwcs.uwstout.edu/parq/intranet/upload/what_quant_test_to_use.pdf. An in-depth decision tree that takes into consideration sample size, variable

type, and normality of sample distribution. Recommends specific types of correlation and regression based on the data.

- William M. K. Trochim, "Selecting Statistics," Social Research Methods, accessed February 8, 2018, www.socialresearchmethods.net/selstat/ssstart.htm. An interactive decision tree that starts with identifying how many variables you have. Includes a glossary and references.
- Institute for Digital Research and Education, "Choosing the Correct Statistical Test in SAS, Stata, SPSS and R," University of California at Los Angeles, 2017, https://stats.idre.ucla.edu/other/mult-pkg/whatstat/. Guidelines for selecting a statistical analysis with the assumption that you are working with statistical software (i.e., SAS, Stata, SPSS, or R).
- Jeremy Stangroom, "Which Statistical Test Should I Use?," Social Science Statistics, 2018, www.socscistatistics.com/tests/what_stats_test_wizard.aspx. An interactive decision tree that begins with a series of questions, then provides recommendations for statistical tests based on your responses to those questions.

Write Your Analysis Plan

Purpose

As you may have noticed throughout this book, there are a number of decision points involved in the analytics process. This makes it critical to have a clear plan guiding you through the process of summarizing and describing your data and testing your hypotheses. Having a clear analysis plan will ensure both that you don't forget any steps and that you have documentation of how you found your results. This can be particularly helpful when you have multiple people working on a project, anticipate needing to refer back to the results at a future point in time, or need to replicate the same analyses with the current or future data sets. The purpose of this appendix is to provide a checklist of the elements you should include in your analysis plan.

Instructions

The checklist is designed to be sequential, although some variation in the order of operations can occur. Keep in mind that some steps may not be necessary for you to complete, and skip over these as appropriate. As you work through your analyses, be sure to keep a record of everything you did and why. In the end, you want to have a methodology document that would allow someone with little to no knowledge of your research and analysis plan to replicate the steps you took and achieve the same outcomes with your data.

Check off each task as it is completed. Before you begin the analysis plan, be sure you have developed your research questions and hypotheses, and identified the variables needed for analyses. Appendices F and G are great tools to ensure that you have what you need to build your analysis plan.

- ☐ Get organized.
  - ☐ Identify your data source(s) (refer to your answers in Appendix F).
  - ☐ List analyses you plan to conduct (refer to Appendix G to help you decide on a statistical test).
  - ☐ Identify tools you'll need to conduct the analyses (e.g., Excel, R).
  - ☐ State the purpose and objective of each analysis.
  - ☐ Write a brief summary of how each objective will be addressed through your analyses.
  - ☐ List the variables you will need for each analysis.
  - ☐ Identify your population (i.e., the entire pool of individuals or groups from which your sample is drawn).
  - ☐ Identify your sample, including any subsets you may want to analyze.
- ☐ Clean your data.
  - ☐ Establish and record data cleaning rules.
  - ☐ Recode variables.
  - ☐ Rename labels and variables.
  - ☐ Identify and remove duplicate cases (i.e., an individual who appears in your data more than once).
  - ☐ Identify and address missing data.
  - ☐ Identify and address outliers (e.g., run z-scores, look at frequency distributions).
  - ☐ Quality check (QC) variables (e.g., typos, values within appropriate range, codes reflect correct labels).
  - ☐ Identify variables with little to no variance.
  - ☐ Transform variables.

☐ Run your analyses.
  ☐ Ensure remaining data have a large enough sample size for the analysis you would like to run (e.g., run descriptive statistics).
  ☐ Apply filters or select cases you need in your analysis if you are analyzing a specific subset of your data. *Note:* Remember to remove the filters when you are not using them and make note of your decisions.
  ☐ Run frequencies on variables of interest.
    ☐ Record *n*.
    ☐ Record output.
    ☐ Create a visual representation of the output.
  ☐ Run descriptive statistics on variables of interest.
    ☐ Record *n*.
    ☐ Record output.
    ☐ Create a visual representation of the output.
  ☐ Run additional analyses (e.g., correlation, ANOVA, regression).
    ☐ Record *n*.
    ☐ Record output.
    ☐ Create a visual representation of the output.
    ☐ Identify highly correlated variables.
  ☐ Record your methodology.
    ☐ Provide definitions or explanations of each variable (i.e., a data dictionary).
    ☐ Describe the cleaning steps.
    ☐ Describe how you handled missing data, outliers, and other data conventions.
    ☐ Describe any inclusion and exclusion criteria.
    ☐ Describe the analyses you ran and why.
    ☐ Describe your sample, your population, and any stratification you used.
    ☐ Describe any models you used (if you ran any regression analyses).
    ☐ Document any variations in the analyses run versus the initial analysis plan and the justification for why.
    ☐ Save your methodology for future access.

☐ Report your findings.
  ☐ Compile your outcomes.
  ☐ Relate outcomes to the initial hypotheses.
  ☐ Relate outcomes to the impact on the business.
  ☐ Determine if there are additional analyses you would like to run and repeat steps above as needed.
  ☐ Create a report of your findings (refer to Appendix I to help you get organized).

Summarize Your Findings

Purpose

In Chapter 7, Jen took a step back to summarize the findings based on each data source. This step can help identify where your findings are conflicting or consistent. It will also help you start to build a complete and integrated story that you can communicate to others. The purpose of this appendix is to help you summarize your findings across data sources. This is also a great opportunity to evaluate the story emerging across sources and redefine the problem.

Instructions

After running the analyses you identified in Appendices G and H, you should now have a set of findings. Use Steps 1 and 2 to make sense of what you have so far. In Step 3, redefine your problem statement and identify the next steps. Remember that just as Jen had to work iteratively throughout the story, you may too. It's not uncommon that analyses yield as many questions as they do answers. Don't be surprised if you need to collect more information even this far into the process.

Step 1. Summarize the findings from each data source.

List each of your data sources in the first column. In the second column, succinctly state your conclusion(s) from that data source. Refer back to Chapter 7 for an example.

Dataset	Findings

Step 2. Look across datasets.

Review your findings across datasets from the table in Step 1. What do you notice? Where are there inconsistencies? What story is emerging?

_____

_____

_____

_____

_____

_____

_____

_____

Step 3. Redefine the problem.

In Chapter 7, you learned that analytics can help you identify the gap between the presenting problem and the real issue. Review your findings. Based on what you're seeing across all of your data sources, write a new problem statement.

_____

_____

_____

_____

_____

_____

_____

_____

Step 4. Identify gaps and next steps.

Now that you've redefined the problem in Step 3, how well do your analyses align? If you're lucky, you've collected and analyzed all the information you need to address the problem. If not, what's missing? How can you fill the gap?

_____

_____

_____

_____

_____

_____

_____

_____

J

Tell Your Story

Purpose

In Chapter 8, Jen used storyboarding as a tool to help her prepare for her presentation to her stakeholders. Communicating data to stakeholders or lay persons can be challenging. Storyboarding is a useful way to make sure your data findings fit into a broader story. Very few people enjoy sitting through a data dump. Stories are most impactful when they are made of both visualizations and words. This combination can ensure that stakeholders understand the data findings and actionable recommendations that you make based on those findings. The purpose of this appendix is to help you translate your findings into a story you can use to communicate to your stakeholders.

Instructions

Follow Steps 1–6 in this appendix to develop your data story.

Step 1. Set the stage.

Who will be presenting the material? Who is the intended audience? What do you need them to do at the end of the presentation? If it's informational, what do they need to do with the information? Do you need approval? Resources? Keep in mind that you may need something different from different audiences or audience members. You may need more than one story to serve your different audience needs and desired actions.

Title	
Author(s)	
Date	
Intended Audience(s)	

Step 2. Get clear on your purpose.

What is the overall purpose of your story? If you're not clear on your purpose, your audience won't be either. What's the one thing you want your audience to take away? Keep it short. Think back to the reflection in Chapter 8—if you had to get your main idea across in one sentence, what would you say? Make sure that your story supports this overall message and repeat it at least three times throughout your presentation.

_____

_____

_____

_____

Step 3. Identify your key points and headlines.

You've spent a lot of time up to this point collecting and analyzing data. Here's where you extract the insights. What are the key points that support your overall goal or purpose?

_____

_____

_____

_____

Step 4. Develop the story text.

Using the boxes below, create a story for your data with a beginning, middle, and end. Outline the problem and its relevance to the audience as well as the goal of the project. Describe how you assessed or addressed the issue and what you found. Propose a solution and highlight a call to action for your audience. Don't forget to incorporate the key points from Step 3.

_____ _____ _____

_____ _____ _____

_____ _____ _____

_____ _____ _____

_____ _____ _____

Step 5. Add data visualizations to supplement the story text.

Remember that a picture is worth a thousand words—or numbers. Looking back at your storyboard from Step 4, where are you supporting your story with data or results from your analytics? Use Figure J.1 for ideas on how you might turn your data into a visualization when it comes time to create your story.

Step 6. Package and disseminate the story to your stakeholders.

Depending on the purpose and points you want to illustrate through your story, you may choose to give an in-person presentation, present remotely, or disseminate electronically (e.g., email). Consider the various resources available to you (e.g., PowerPoint, Word, Excel, video, infographics) and select the best option based on time, stakeholder, message, and ease of understanding. Refer to Appendix L to determine the best way to package and communicate your plan.

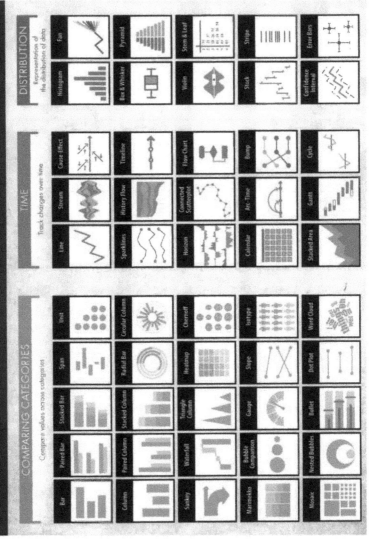

Figure J.1. The Graphic Continuum (part 1 of 2)

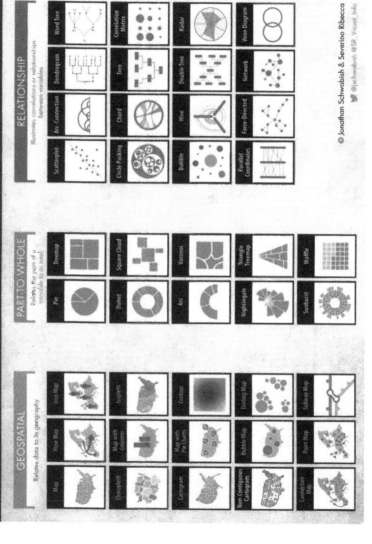

Figure J.1. The Graphic Continuum (part 2 of 2)

K

Plan Your Evaluation

Purpose

In Chapter 9, we described the importance of program evaluation in supporting continuous improvement, stakeholder engagement, and demonstrating impact. Evaluating your solution to the business challenge you started with is a great way to close the circle and ensure analytics continue to feed your decision-making process. The purpose of this appendix is to provide you with a template you can use to develop a way to evaluate how effectively you were able to solve your business challenge.

Instructions

Use this template to describe how you will evaluate the program or solution you developed to address the business challenge.

Evaluation Plan Template
Background

Include a brief description of the context, challenge, and proposed solution or program.

_____

_____

_____

_____

_____

_____

Program Objectives

Briefly describe the strategic goals or objectives of the solution. It can be helpful to assign a number or convention to each to ensure that you have mapped metrics to each of the goals. Provide a brief description of the rationale behind how the solution will address these goals.

_____

_____

_____

_____

_____

_____

Evaluation Roles and Responsibilities

Describe what groups or individuals will be responsible for developing and implementing the evaluation plan.

Group or Individual	Role

Current Stakeholders

Stakeholder is a term used to identify any person or group that is invested in the successful outcome of a project and can directly influence resource allocation. Refer back to your responses in Appendix E to review the stakeholders you identified previously.

Role or Title	Stake or Interest

Program Evaluation Questions

Questions addressed by a program evaluation should reflect the initial program goals. The list should reflect what the current stakeholders view as critical to evaluating its effectiveness. One easy way to ensure alignment between questions and goals is to carry through the numbering convention you used for the goals. For example, Goal 1 might be aligned to Evaluation Questions 1.01, 1.02, and 1.03 and so forth.

Reference Number	Evaluation Question
Program Objective 1	
1.01	
1.02	
...	
Program Objective 2	
2.01	
2.02	
...	

Measures

Use the table below to outline recommendations for measures or metrics that can be used to evaluate the extent to which the program or solution meets the intended goals or objectives. Where possible, baseline measures should be collected and potential unintended consequences should be identified and monitored. Refer to Chapter 9 for an example.

- *Target(s)* refers to your hypothesis (e.g., increase, maintain, decrease) about how the program will impact the measure.
- *Metric Owner* refers to the individual(s) or group(s) responsible for collecting or monitoring the measure.
- *Research Question(s)* refers to the convention associated with the question the measure serves to address (e.g., "1.01").
- *Timeline* refers to the regularity with which you plan to collect the measure (e.g., baseline, quarterly, annually).

When considering what measures to include, Alec Levenson recommends that they meet four criteria he describes using the acronym CARE:[1]

- **Consistent**—The metric is measured consistently over time.
- **Accurate**—There are few or no errors in the data.
- **Reliable**—The data are an accurate approximation of what they are intended to represent.
- **Efficient**—The cost (in time and/or money) of collecting the data is minimal.

Measures that fail to meet these criteria will have limited utility.

Measure or Metric	Target(s)	Metric Source(s)	Metric Owner	Research Question(s)	Timeline

Data Collection, Analysis, and Reporting

Use this section to describe how and how often you will go about collecting, analyzing, and reporting the results of the evaluation. This section should also specify the reporting frequency and how results will be used (e.g., continuous improvement cycles).

_____

_____

_____

_____

_____

_____

Endnote

1. Alec Levenson, *Strategic Analytics: Advancing Strategy Execution and Organizational Effectiveness* (Oakland: Berrett-Koehler Publishers, 2015).

L

Communicate Your Plan

Purpose

The purpose of a communication plan is to maximize the chance of project success by meeting the information needs of your stakeholders. This appendix provides a template for you to use as you develop your communication plan.

Instructions

Use this template to define the communication methods and content necessary to achieve your project goals.

Communication Goals and Objectives

Describe the goals the you want to achieve with the communications plan. These should align with the goals of the evaluation plan you developed in Appendix K.

Stakeholders

List the communication to stakeholders (your audiences). Refer back to Appendix E to review the list you developed.

Name	Title	Role	Communication Need(s)	Comments
Jane Smith	Director, R&D	Client sponsor	Status updates	Willing to serve as internal champion

Key Messages

Identify the key messages you want to communicate about your project.

Communication Matrix

Use this table to identify the vehicles, audience, and frequency you will use to communicate throughout your project. This will need to be a living document that you update throughout the various phases of the project.

Audience	Content	Format	Timing	Resources
Executive sponsor	Milestone update	Email or PPT	Ongoing as needed	Project summary

M

Set Up an Analytics Function

Purpose

No matter the company or HR department, starting the journey toward an effective and efficient HR analytics function can seem daunting. There's no single right way to create and manage an HR analytics function. The role of HR analytics in a company can sit within a variety of departments or act as its own department; whether it be composed of a one-person army or a hundred-person team. For this reason we will refer to the role of HR analytics within a company as the HR analytics function as opposed to a department or group.

Similarly, there is not one ideal profile of analytics that applies to all companies. Every company has unique attributes, goals, and limitations that shape the vision for its analytics function. Recall the HR analytics maturity model from Chapter 4. The model has four levels of analytical capabilities and a variety of components within each level. The level your company strives for will likely be determined by a variety of factors, such as your business challenges, competitive context, resources, and even ambition. Fundamental components such as data accuracy, reporting metrics, and establishing dashboards are helpful (and a necessary precursor to anything more advanced) in every organization. Some companies will go on to strive to build advanced capabilities such as predictive models to further their competitive advantage.

Although there is no single way to establish the right HR analytics function, there are some best practices that can help focus your efforts and resources. The purpose of this appendix is to provide you with a high-level overview of steps you can take to create an analytics function that fits your company—whether you're a team of one or one hundred.

Instructions

Follow the steps in this appendix to help you structure your journey to start an analytics function.

Step 1. Assess the climate.

The first step in building an analytics function is to assess the current state of the organization on relevant factors. One such factor is understanding the appetite for and vision of analytics among your leadership and decision makers. Meet with your leaders to learn more about their expectations and perspectives. Use this information to inform your assessment of the current state. It can also shape the function's future structure and mission. Use the questions below to help you initiate the conversation with your leaders.

- What's your vision for an analytics function? What's the purpose of developing the company's HR analytics capabilities?

  _____

  _____

  _____

- Which leaders should be involved in this process and mentoring the function? What role would they play?

  _____

  _____

  _____

- Who will ultimately be the stakeholders? Who cares about the success of the function and its deliverables?

  _____

  _____

  _____

In addition to understanding the broader vision for analytics in your organization, it's also helpful to consider what's currently working, broken, or lacking. Use the items below to assess your organization's current standing on each factor in your organization today. After each rating, describe what led you to make the rating—what are the specific strengths and challenges you have to work with?

1. My understanding of the vision for the company's analytics function and its purpose is

0	1	2	3	4	5
Nonexistent		Somewhat clear			Completely clear

_____

_____

_____

2. My understanding of whom I should turn to for direction and input while developing and maintaining this function is

0	1	2	3	4	5
Nonexistent		Somewhat clear			Completely clear

_____

_____

_____

3. The stakeholders in the success of the HR analytics function are

0	1	2	3	4	5
Unidentified		Somewhat clear			Completely clear

_____

_____

_____

4. The definitions and guidelines and procedures to collect, enter, and securely manage data in our systems are

0	1	2	3	4	5
Nonexistent		Somewhat clear			Completely clear

_____

_____

_____

5. The reports and metrics HR creates and disseminates to leadership are

0	1	2	3	4	5
Nonexistent		Somewhat valuable			Highly valuable

_____

_____

_____

6. The technical resources dedicated to analytics are

0	1	2	3	4	5
Nonexistent		Somewhat sufficent			Extensive

_____

_____

_____

7. The people resources dedicated to analytics are

0	1	2	3	4	5
Nonexistent		Somewhat sufficient			Extensive

_____

_____

_____

8. My understanding of the business processes that impact the data we use is

0	1	2	3	4	5
Nonexistent		Somewhat clear			Completely clear

_____

_____

_____

9. What other factors should be considered?

_____

_____

_____

10. What will be the most challenging factor? Why?

_____

_____

_____

Step 2. Target an approach.

Data used in HR analytics will come in multiple forms and from multiple sources that don't always integrate well. This means you need to be resourceful and get creative when gathering information. Silos and lack of communication can hinder your ability to find obscure data sources or understand important business processes. Creating an HR metrics glossary—like the one in Appendix D—and a data dictionary (also known as data definition matrix or a metadata repository) can help you consolidate and clarify information across data owners and users.

Different data stakeholders have different interests in the data. Multiple groups are often responsible for different portions of the data creation and management processes. A change in one part of the process can have major downstream implications for other stakeholders. Use the tips in this step to help you mitigate this issue.

Tip 1. Develop a governance committee.

One way to address data integrity issues is to develop a well-defined data structure and document standards. Multiple stakeholders and data owners means you'll need to get help from others. Create a committee with at least one representative from each group of stakeholders. The committee should meet regularly to discuss topics such as implementing data standard guidelines (e.g., creating a data dictionary), documenting processes (e.g., develop process maps for employee separations), and sharing relevant project updates and concerns (e.g., IT systems updates).

Part of establishing your committee will involve developing a charter. Use the template below to think through what the committee charter should include.

- Background (What sparked the need for this committee? Who requested it?)

  _____

  _____

  _____

- Goal (What is the ultimate goal of this group? What will success look like?)

  _____

  _____

  _____

- Scope (What business processes or components will the committee oversee? What are the expectations?)

  _____

  _____

  _____

- Committee members and roles (Who's involved and why? What unique attribute do they offer? Who's the committee chair? Which leaders will sponsor this committee?)

  _____

  _____

  _____

Tip 2. Generate quick wins.

If you are just getting acquainted with data, start with the basics—execute some quick wins to demonstrate the function's value. It's easy to underestimate the amount of time needed to execute a data project. Start out small to give yourself an opportunity to work out the kinks in the new function.

If you've been using the appendices in this book to apply analytics in your organization, you've already completed several activities to help you identify your next quick win. Use the challenges and available data you identified in Appendix C, as well as the metrics table in Appendix D to identify the quick win(s) you could execute within each of the timeframes below.

- One week

  _____

  _____

  _____

- One month

  _____

  _____

  _____

- One quarter

  _____

  _____

  _____

Tip 3. Assess your resources.

Now you are ready to get into the details—including figuring out what resources you have available to you. Use the lens of business, people, and data that was explained in Chapter 2 to assess your resources.

- What processes are supporting or prohibiting your efforts?
- Do you have the right people in place or will you need to outsource some skills and roles?
- Is the company's data accurate and reliable?
- What tools are available to conduct analyses (e.g., HRIS, Excel, SPSS)?

_____

_____

_____

This assessment can be among the responsibilities of the data governance committee described in Tip 1.

- Business

_____

_____

_____

- People

_____

_____

_____

- Data

_____

_____

_____

Step 3. Define the strategy.

Steps 1 and 2 helped you lay an initial foundation for the design of the function. Now, it's time to build on it to shape the future. What will this department look like in one, three, or five years? How will you achieve this? Use the space below to draft a strategy statement.

_____

_____

_____

Step 4. Build a team.

Think of building an HR Analytics team as building a project team just like Jen did. The big difference is that the analytics team will continue to work together, likely on a variety of projects. High-functioning analytics teams are usually multidisciplinary. As you saw in Jen's story, it's more than just numbers and formulas. The team needs to incorporate a variety of skills and perspectives.

As I noted above, there's no magic number of people for an analytics function. Instead, it's more important to focus on having the right skills and competencies, as discussed in Appendix A. In general, you should staff your analytics function with individuals who can advocate for data's utility, gather meaningful data, conduct sound analyses, and translate the results into actionable insights that will help leaders make decisions. Who within your organization might fit into each of these four areas?

- Data advocacy (promote the value and importance of the data)

  _____

  _____

  _____

- Data gathering (identify the best data sources, tools, and methods of data collection)

  _____

  _____

  _____

- Data analysis (apply the appropriate analytics and identify useful insights in the results)

  _____

  _____

  _____

- Evidence-based decision-making (create and propose effective solutions based on insights)

  _____

  _____

  _____

Step 5. Identify a project management approach.

In a typical analytics function, you will have to work on multiple projects at the same time. This might mean that you're not just focusing on R&D's turnover issue, you're also developing a workforce plan to inform next year's budget and evaluating the effectiveness of your recruiting strategy simultaneously. As you might imagine, that can get pretty hairy. A strong project management (PM) approach will be key to your function's success.

There are many PM methodologies and tools you can use to help you manage all of the demands you'll encounter. Use the resources available in the bibliography and resource section of this book to learn more about what's right for you. Because you're starting a new function, you'll probably be learning as you go. An agile PM approach can be very useful when you're facing unclear or changing expectations. Agile PM uses small work cycles, or _sprints,_ within the project to complete individual project components. This iterative approach allows for midstream changes and flexibility. Steps in this approach can occur simultaneously, which can support a quick turnaround.

Step 6. Communicate with your stakeholders.

Not everyone in your organization will be familiar with an HR analytics function, its products, and the value it can create. In addition, HR isn't the only function with a data skills gap. Some stakeholders might struggle to understand how to use and interpret the data (e.g., metrics on a dashboard). Consider launching a campaign to promote analytics and HR data, or providing additional support when new reports or analyses are released. Example strategies to consider in your campaign are provided below.

- **Distribute a monthly educational communication.** Each month, highlight a different metric—define and describe it and inform the audience of its recent measure. Let's use headcount as an example.
    - o Define headcount: What employees are included?
    - o Describe its relevance to business: How has headcount aligned with business performance?
    - o Report the current state: What is the company's actual active headcount as of the end of the quarter? How has this fluctuated in the last twelve months?
- **Hold supplemental calls.** Offer supplemental conference calls with the audience of a report. During the call, walk through key highlights of the new reports. Include time for audience questions. Let's use a quarterly HR dashboard as an example.
    - o After disseminating the dashboard, schedule a conference call and invite everyone who receives the report.
    - o Before the call, identify and prepare key points based on insights you can extract from the metrics. What are the most drastic and important changes since the last report?
    - o During the call, quickly present an overview of the report's metrics or data, then review the key points you created before the call. Open up the conversation for their questions and concerns. This is a great way to open the lines of communication, and collect feedback that can improve the

usefulness of your reports while building the department's visibility.

What strategies will you include to communicate with stakeholders about the new function?

_____

_____

_____

How will you help support end-users to ensure they get the full benefits of the function's products?

_____

_____

_____

Step 7. Create your organization's roadmap.

Remember that there are many ways to develop your company's analytics function. Use the information from this appendix and the additional resources at the end of this book to help you create your own roadmap, like the one in Figure M.1. List the steps you will take and the roadblocks (i.e., challenges) you anticipate along the way. You might have more or fewer points on your map—this figure is just a way to get you started. Use the space below the map to expand on the steps or roadblocks you identify in the figure.

Step 1

_____

_____

_____

Roadblock 1

_____

_____

_____

Step 2

_____

_____

_____

_____

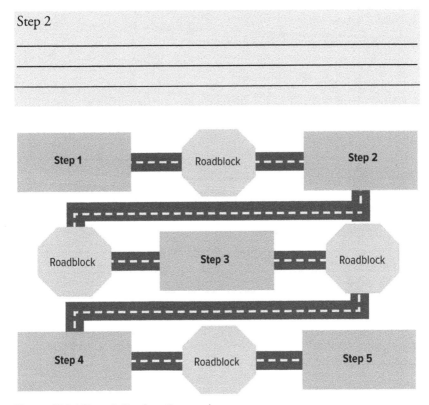

Figure M.1. HR analytics function roadmap

Roadblock 2

_____

_____

_____

Step 3

_____

_____

_____

Roadblock 3

_____
_____
_____

Step 4

_____
_____
_____

Roadblock 4

_____
_____
_____

Step 5

_____
_____
_____

Additional steps

_____
_____
_____

Additional roadblocks

_____
_____
_____

Bibliography

American Statistical Association. "Statisticians Don't Need a Crystal Ball to Predict the Future." ThisIsStatistics.org, April 28, 2016. http://thisisstatistics.org/statisticians-dont-need-a-crystal-ball-to-predict-the-future/.

Anderson, Chris. *TED Talks: The Official Guide to Public Speaking.* New York: Houghton Mifflin Harcourt Publishing Company, 2016.

Antman, Elliott M., Joseph Lau, Bruce Kupelnick, Frederick Mosteller, and Thomas C. Chalmers. "A Comparison of Results of Meta-analyses of Randomized Control Trials and Recommendations of Clinical Experts: Treatments for Myocardial Infarction." *Journal of the American Medical Association* 268, no. 2 (1992): 240–48.

Applebaum, Steven H., and Rammie Kamal. "An Analysis of the Utilization and Effectiveness of Non-financial Incentives in Small Business." *Journal of Management Development* 19, no. 9 (2000): 723–63.

Ayres, Ian. *Super Crunchers: Why Thinking-by-Numbers is the New Way to Be Smart."* New York: Bantam Books, 2008.

Barends, Eric, Denise Rousseau, and Rob Briner. *Evidence-Based Management: The Basic Principles.* Amsterdam: Center for Evidence-Based Management, 2014. https://www.cebma.org/wp-content/uploads/Evidence-Based-Practice-The-Basic-Principles.pdf.

Bennett, Ty. *The Power of Storytelling: The Art of Influential Communication.* American Fork, UT: Sound Concepts Inc., 2013.

Benson, Buster. "Cognitive Bias Cheat Sheet." *Better Humans*, September 1, 2016. https://betterhumans.coach.me/cognitive-bias-cheat-sheet-55a472476b18.

Berinato, Scott. "Visualizations That Really Work." *Harvard Business Review*, June 2016. https://hbr.org/2016/06/visualizations-that-really-work.

Bersin, Josh. "The Datafication of HR." *Deloitte Review*, no. 14 (January 17, 2014). https://www2.deloitte.com/insights/us/en/deloitte-review/issue-14/dr14-datafication-of-hr.html.

Bladt, Jeff, and Bob Filbin. "Know the Difference between Your Data and Your Metrics." *Harvard Business Review* 4 (2013). https://hbr.org/2013/03/know-the-difference-between-yo.

Borman, Walter C. "Consistency of Rating Accuracy and Rating Errors in the Judgment of Human Performance." *Organizational Behavior and Human Performance* 20, no. 2 (1977): 238–52.

Cable, Daniel M., and Timothy A. Judge. "Pay Preferences and Job Search Decisions: A Person-Organization Fit Perspective." *Personnel Psychology* 47, no. 2 (1994): 317–48

Campbell, John P., Rondey A. McCloy, Scott H. Oppler, and Christopher E. Sager. "A Theory of Performance." In *Frontiers in Industrial/Organizational Psychology: Personnel Selection and Classification*, ed. N. Schmitt and W. C. Borman, 35–71. San Francisco: Jossey-Bass, 1993.

Cappelli, Peter. "There's No Such Thing as Big Data in HR." *Harvard Business Review*, July 7, 2017. http://www.hbr.org/2017/06/theres-no-such-thing-as-big-data-in-hr?lipi=urn%3Ali%3Apage%3Ad_flagship3_pulse_read%3Bvw Y6ZNEzRSO%2Baal%2BV7XiBQ%3D%3D.

Cerasoli, Christopher P., Jessica M. Nicklin, and Michael T. Ford. "Intrinsic Motivation and Extrinsic Incentives Jointly Predict Performance: A 40-Year Meta-analysis." *Psychological Bulletin* 140, no. 4 (2014): 980–1008.

Cohen, Jacob. *Statistical Power Analysis for the Behavioral Sciences*. 2nd ed. Hillsdale, NJ: Lawrence Erlbaum, 1988.

Colquitt, Alan. *Next Generation Performance Management: The Triumph of Science over Myth and Superstition*. Charlotte, NC: Information Age Publishing Inc., 2017.

Cortina, Jose M., and Ronald S. Landis, eds. *Modern Research Methods for the Study of Behavior in Organizations*. London: Routledge, 2014.

Dastani, Mehdi. 'The Role of Visual Perception in Data Visualization." *Journal of Visual Languages & Computing* 13, no. 6 (2002): 601–22.

Davenport, Thomas H. "10 Kinds of Stories to Tell with Data." *Harvard Business Review*, May 5, 2014. https://hbr.org/2014/05/10-kinds-of-stories-to-tell-with-data.

Deci, Edward L., and Richard M. Ryan. "A Motivational Approach to Self: Integration in Personality." In *Perspectives on Motivation*, vol. 38 of *Nebraska Symposium on Motivation*, edited by Richard A. Dienstbier, 237–88. Lincoln: University of Nebraska Press, 1991.

Dietvorst, Berkeley J., Joseph P. Simmons, and Cade Massey. "Overcoming Algorithm Aversion: People Will Use Imperfect Algorithms If They Can (Even Slightly) Modify Them." *Management Science*, November 4, 2016. https://doi.org/10.1287/mnsc.2016.2643.

EBSCO Help. "EBSCOhost Advanced Searching – Tutorial." YouTube, August 19, 2015. https://www.youtube.com/watch?v=kT1kzWfWxiE.

Economist Intelligence Unit. *Gut and Gigabytes: Capitalising on the Art and Science in Decision Making.* London: PwC, 2014. https://www.pwc.com/gx/en/issues/data-and-analytics/big-decisions-survey/assets/big-decisions2014.pdf.

———. *Use of Workforce Analytics for Competitive Advantage.* Alexandria: Society for Human Resource Management, 2016.

Edmondson, Amy C. "Managing the Risk of Learning: Psychological Safety in Work Teams." In *International Handbook of Organizational Teamwork and Co-operative Learning,* edited by Michael West, Dean Tjosvold, and Ken Smith, 255–76. Chichester, Eng.: John Wiley and Sons, 2003.

———. "Psychological Safety and Learning Behavior in Work Teams." *Administrative Science Quarterly* 44, no. 2 (1999): 350–83.

Epic Tutorials for iOS & Android Filmmaking. "How to Google Like a Pro! Top 10 Google Search Tips & Tricks." YouTube, April 5, 2010. https://www.youtube.com/watch?v=R0DQfwc72PM.

Ferrar, Jonathan. "Data Storytelling: Know Your Audience." HR Zone, October 25, 2017. https://www.hrzone.com/engage/employees/data-storytelling-know-your-audience.

Few, Stephen. *Information Dashboard Design: Displaying Data for At-a-Glance Monitoring.* Burlingame, CA: Analytics Press, 2013.

Filipkowski, Jenna. *Insightful HR: Integrating Quality Data for Better Talent Decisions.* Human Capital Institute Research, April 28, 2015. http://pcdn4.hci.org/files/field_content_file/2015%20Oracle.pdf.

Frick, Walter. "Here's Why People Trust Human Judgment over Algorithms." *Harvard Business Review,* February 27, 2015. https://hbr.org/2015/02/heres-why-people-trust-human-judgment-over-algorithms.

Future of StoryTelling. "Empathy, Neurochemistry, and the Dramatic Arc: Paul Zak at the Future of StoryTelling 2012." YouTube, October 3, 2012. https://www.youtube.com/watch?v=q1a7tiA1Qzo.

Future Work Centre. *"Think like a Scientist!" Finding Out What Works in What Way and for Whom.* White paper. 2016. http://www.futureworkcentre.com/wp-content/uploads/2016/09/Think-like-a-scientist-white-paper.pdf.

Gagné, Marylène, and Edward L. Deci. "Self-Determination Theory and Work Motivation." *Journal of Organizational Behavior* 26, no. 4 (2005): 331–62.

Gallo, Amy. "A Refresher on Regression Analysis." *Harvard Business Review,* November 4, 2015. https://hbr.org/2015/11/a-refresher-on-regression-analysis.

———. "A Refresher on Statistical Significance." *Harvard Business Review,* February 16, 2016. https://hbr.org/2016/02/a-refresher-on-statistical-significance.

Garb, Howard N., and William M. Grove. "On the Merits of Clinical Judgment: Comment." *American Psychologist* 60, no. 6 (2005): 658–59.

Gorman, C. Allen, and Joan R. Rentsch. "Evaluating Frame-of-Reference Rater Training Effectiveness using Performance Schema Accuracy." *Journal of Applied Psychology* 94, no. 5 (2009): 1336–44.

Grande, Todd. "Pretest and Posttest Analysis Using Excel." YouTube, December 2, 2014. https://www.youtube.com/watch?v=LZxaMmCZFm4.

Griffeth, Rodger W., Peter W. Hom, and Stefan Gaertner. "A Meta-analysis of Antecedents and Correlates of Employee Turnover: Update, Moderator Tests, and Research Implications for the Next Millennium." *Journal of Management* 26, no. 3 (2000): 463–88.

Guastello, Steven J., H. Boeh, H. Gorin, S. Huschen, N. E. Peters, M. Fabisch, and K. Poston. "Cusp Catastrophe Models for Cognitive Workload and Fatigue: A Comparison of Seven Task Types." *Nonlinear Dynamics, Psychology, and Life Sciences* 17, no. 1 (January 2013): 23–47.

Guastello, Steven J., and David W. McGee. "Mathematical Modeling of Fatigue in Physically Demanding Jobs." *Journal of Mathematical Psychology* 31, no. 1 (1987): 248–69.

Guion, Robert M. *Assessment, Measurement, and Prediction for Personnel Decisions.* 2nd ed. London: Routledge, 2011.

Gupta, Aarti, Apoorv Anand, Christine Garcia, Lilianna Bagnoli, Sahaj Talwar, Shilpa Arora, Udit Poddar, Uttara Rajasekar, and Vasavi Ayasomayajula. *The Ultimate Guide to Basic Data Cleaning.* N.p.: SocialCops, accessed December 23, 2018. https://cdn2.hubspot.net/hubfs/2287011/ebook_data_cleaning/Free%20Ebook%20-%20The%20Ultimate%20Guide%20to%20Basic%20Data%20Cleaning.pdf.

Hackman, J. Richard, and Greg R. Oldham. "Development of the Job Diagnostic Survey." *Journal of Applied Psychology* 60, no. 2 (1975): 159–70.

Herzberg, Frederick I. *Work and the Nature of Man.* Cleveland: World Publishing Company, 1966.

Holtom, Brooks, Caren B. Goldberg, David G. Allen, and Mark A. Clark. "How Today's Shocks Predict Tomorrow's Leaving." *Journal of Business and Psychology* 32, no. 1 (2017): 59–71.

Hu, Jia, Berrin Erdogan, Kaifeng Jiang, Talya N. Bauer, and Songbo Liu. "Leader Humility and Team Creativity: The Role of Team Information Sharing, Psychological Safety, and Power Distance." *Journal of Applied Psychology*, advance online publication. http://dx.doi.org/10.1037/apl0000277.

Jones, Rebecca J., Stephen A. Woods, and Yyves R. F. Guillaume. "The Effectiveness of Workplace Coaching: A Meta-analysis of Learning and Performance Outcomes from Coaching." *Journal of Occupational and Organizational Psychology*, 89, no. 2 (2015): 249–77.

Kahneman, Daniel, and Amos Tversky. "Prospect Theory: An Analysis of Decision under Risk." *Econometrica* 47 (1979): 263–91.

Kalish, Yuval. "Harnessing the Power of Social Network Analysis to Explain Organizational Phenomena," in Cortina and Landis, *Modern Research Methods*, 99–135.

Lacerenza, Christina N., Denise L. Reyes, Shannon L. Marlow, Dana I. Joseph, and Eduordo Salas. "Leadership Training Design, Delivery, and Implementation: A Meta-analysis." *Journal of Applied Psychology* 27, no. 12 (July 2017): 1686–718.

Lane, David M. "Normal Distribution," in *Hyperstat Online*. N.p.: N.p., 2001. http://davidmlane.com/hyperstat/normal_distribution.html.

Laney, Doug. "3D Data Management: Controlling Data Volume, Velocity, and Variety." *META Group* 6 (2001). https://blogs.gartner.com/doug-laney/files/2012/01/ad949-3D-Data-Management-Controlling-Data-Volume-Velocity-and-Variety.pdf.

Latham, Gary. *Becoming the Evidence-Based Manager: Making the Science of Management Work for You.* Boston: Davies-Black, 2009.

Levenson, Alec. *Strategic Analytics: Advancing Strategy Execution and Organizational Effectiveness.* Oakland: Berrett-Koehler Publishers, 2015.

Lewis, Michael. *Moneyball: The Art of Winning the Unfair Game.* New York: W.W. Norton and Company, 2003.

Lewis-Beck, Colin, and Michael Lewis-Beck. *Applied Regression: An Introduction.* 2nd ed. Newbury Park, CA: Sage Publications, 2016.

Liang, Jian, Crystal I. C. Farh, and Jing-Lih Farh. "Psychological Antecedents of Promotive and Prohibitive Voice: A Two-Wave Examination." *Academy of Management Journal* 55, no. 1 (2012): 71–92.

Lunenburg, Fred C. "Performance Appraisal: Methods and Rating Errors." *International Journal of Scholarly Academic Intellectual Diversity* 14, no. 1 (2012): 1–9.

Machlean, Kyle, Lauren E. Cipriano, and Gregory S. Zaric. "Descriptive Statistics in Microsoft Excel." *Harvard Business Review*, June 29, 2016.

Maslow, Abraham H. *The Farther Reaches of Human Nature.* New York: Viking Press, 1971.

Meehl, Paul E. *Clinical versus Statistical Prediction: A Theoretical Analysis and a Review of the Evidence.* Minneapolis: University of Minnesota, 1954.

Newman, Thomas B. "The Power of Stories over Statistics: Lessons from Neonatal Jaundice and Infant Airplane Safety." In *Narrative Research in Health and Illness*, edited by Brian Hurwitz, Trisha Greenhalfh, and Vieda Skultans, 257–76. London: Wiley, 2004.

Nisbet, Robert, and Gary Miner. *Handbook of Statistical Analysis and Data Mining Applications.* Cambridge, MA: Academic Press, 2009.

O'Hara, Carolyn. "How to Tell a Great Story." *Harvard Business Review*, July 30, 2014. https://hbr.org/2014/07/how-to-tell-a-great-story.

Pennings, Johannes M., and Jaana Woiceshyn. "A Typology of Organizational Control and Its Metaphors." *Research in the Sociology of Organizations* 5, no. 73 (1987): 73–104.

Ployhart, Robert, and Youngsang Kim. "Dynamic Longitudinal Growth Modeling." In Cortina and Landis, *Modern Research Methods*, 63–98.

Rousseau, Denise M., and Eric G. R. Barends. "Becoming an Evidence-Based HR Practitioner." *Human Resource Management Journal* 21, no. 3 (2011): 221–35. https://doi.org/10.1111/j.1748-8583.2011.00173.x.

Ryan, Richard M., Edward L. Deci, and Wendy S. Grolnick. "Autonomy, Relatedness, and the Self: Their Relation to Development and Psychopathology." In *Theory and Methods*, vol. 1 of *Developmental Psychology*, edited by Dante Cicchetti and Donald J. Cohen, 618–55. New York: Wiley, 1995.

Rynes, Sara L. "The Research-Practice Gap in I/O Psychology and Related Fields: Challenges and Potential Solutions." In *The Oxford Handbook of Organizational Psychology*, vol. 1, edited by Steve W. J. Kozlowski, 409–52. Oxford: Oxford University Press, 2012.

SAS. *Data Visualization Techniques: From Basics to Big Data with SAS® Visual Analytics*. White paper. Cary, NC: SAS, 2017.

Shaper, Shannon. "How Many Interviews Does It Take to Hire a Googler?" *re:Work* (blog), April 4, 2017. https://rework.withgoogle.com/blog/google-rule-of-four/.

Society for Human Resource Management. "Developing and Sustaining High-Performance Work Teams." July 23, 2015. https://www.shrm.org/resourcesandtools/tools-and-samples/toolkits/pages/developingandsustaininghigh-performanceworkteams.aspx.

———. "How to Conduct an Employee Focus Group." June 19, 2015. https://www.shrm.org/resourcesandtools/tools-and-samples/how-to-guides/pages/conduct-employee-focus-group.aspx.

———. "Metrics List," Excel document, accessed February 9, 2018, https://www.shrm.org/ResourcesAndTools/business-solutions/Documents/Metrics-List.xlsx.

———. "Stay Interview Questions." Accessed February 6, 2018. https://www.shrm.org/resourcesandtools/tools-and-samples/hr-forms/pages/stayinterviewquestions.aspx.

Spradlin, Dwayne. "Are You Solving the Right Problem?" *Harvard Business Review*, September 2012. https://hbr.org/2012/09/are-you-solving-the-right-problem.

Support. "Change Management and Change Management Models." RapidBi, May 10, 2016. https://rapidbi.com/changemanagement/.

Thorndike, Edward L. "A Constant Error in Psychological Ratings." *Journal of Applied Psychology* 4, no. 1 (1920): 25–29.

Trank, Christine Quinn, Sara L. Rynes, and Robert D. Bretz. "Attracting Applicants in the War for Talent: Differences in Work Preferences among High Achievers." *Journal of Business and Psychology* 16, no. 3 (2002): 331–45.

Wang-Audia, Wendy. "Talent Analytics: From Small Data to Big Data." Research bulletin, Bersin by Deloitte (2013).

Waters, Shonna. "Learn How to Handle the Unexpected Events that Trigger Turnover." *HR Magazine*, October 2017. https://www.shrm.org/hr-today/news/hr-magazine/1017/Pages/learn-how-to-handle-the-unexpected-events-that-trigger-turnover.aspx.

Webb, Thomas L., and Paschal Sheeran. "Does Changing Behavioral Intentions Engender Behavior Change? A Meta-analysis of the Experimental Evidence." *Psychological Bulletin* 132, no. 2 (2006): 249–68.

Additional Reference Materials

Topics

HR Metrics

HR Metrics Service. *Standards and Glossary*. Version 9.4, January 2018. www.hrmetricsservice.org/wp-content/uploads/2013/07/HR-Metrics-Service-Standards-and-Glossary-v9.4.pdf.

HR Business Process Outsourcing. *Human Resources Reporting and Analytics Priorities Survey: Survey Highlights 2011*. London: Aon Hewitt, 2011. www.aon.com/attachments/thought-leadership/HR_Reporting_and_Analytics_Priorities.pdf.

van Vulpen, Erik. "11 Key HR Metrics." *Analytics in HR* (blog), August 2017. www.analyticsinhr.com/blog/11-key-hr-metrics/.

———. "What Is an HR Dashboard and HR Report? Examples, Visuals and a How-To." *Analytics in HR* (blog), March 2017. www.analyticsinhr.com/blog/hr-reporting-hr-report-hr-dashboard/.

Overview of Analytics

Barrenechea, Mark. "Big Data: Big Hype?" *CIO Network* (blog), *Forbes*, June 27, 2014, www.forbes.com/sites/ciocentral/2013/02/04/big-data-big-hype/.

Bartlet, Randy. *A Practitioner's Guide to Business Analytics: Using Data Analysis Tools to Improve Your Organization's Decision Making and Strategy*. New York: McGraw-Hill, 2013.

Bersin, Josh. "Big Data in Human Resources: Talent Analytics (People Analytics) Comes of Age." *Forbes Magazine*, February 17, 2013. www.forbes.com/sites/joshbersin/2013/02/17/bigdata-in-human-resources-talent-analytics-comes-of-age/.

Collins, Laurence, David R. Fineman, and Akio Tsuchida. "People Analytics: Recalculating the Route." *Deloitte Insights*, February 28, 2017. www.deloitte.com/insights/us/en/focus/human-capital-trends/2017/people-analytics-in-hr.html.

DeRose, Chris. "How Google Uses Data to Build a Better Worker." *Atlantic,* October 7, 2013. www.theatlantic.com/business/archive/2013/10/ how-google-uses-data-to-build-a-better-worker/280347/.

Donoho, David. "50 Years of Data Science." Paper based on a presentation given at the Tukey Centennial Workshop, Princeton, NJ, September 18, 2015. http://courses.csail.mit.edu/18.337/2015/docs/50YearsDataScience.pdf.

EMC Education Services, ed. *Data Science and Big Data Analytics: Discovering, Analyzing, Visualizing and Presenting Data.* Hoboken, NJ: Wiley, 2015.

Gandomi, Amir, and Murtaza Haider. "Beyond the Hype: Big Data Concepts, Methods, and Analytics." *International Journal of Information Management* 35, no. 2 (2015): 137–44. https://doi.org/10.1016/j.ijinfomgt.2014.10.007.

George, Gerard, Martine R. Haas, and Alex Pentland. "Big Data and Management." *Academy of Management Journal* 57, no. 2 (2014): 321–326. https://doi.org/10.5465/amj.2014.4002.

Guzzo, Richard A., Alexis A. Fink, Eden King, Scott Tonidandel, and Ronald S. Landis. "Big Data Recommendations for Industrial–Organizational Psychology." *Industrial and Organizational Psychology* 8, no. 4 (2015): 491–508. https://doi.org/10.1017/iop.2015.40.

Landers, Richard, Alexis A. Fink, and Andrew B. Collmus. "Using Big Data to Enhance Staffing: Vast Untapped Resources or Tempting Honeypot?" In *Handbook of Employee Selection,* 2nd ed., ed. James L. Farr and Nancy Thomas Tippins, 949–966. New York: Routledge, 2017.

Levenson, Alec. "The Promise of Big Data for HR." *People and Strategy* 26, no. 4 (2014): 22–26.

Marshall, Anthony, Stefan Mueck, and Rebecca Shockley. "How Leading Organizations Use Big Data and Analytics to Innovate." *Strategy and Leadership* 43, no. 5 (2015): 32–39. https://doi.org/10.1108/ sl-06-2015-0054.

McAfee, Andrew, and Erik Brynjolfsson. "Big Data: The Management Revolution." *Harvard Business Review,* October 2012. www.hbr. org/2012/10/big-data-the-management-revolution.

Provost, Foster, and Tom Fawcett. *Data Science for Business: What You Need to Know about Data Mining and Data-Analytic Thinking.* Sebastopol, CA: O'Reilly Media, 2013.

Russell, Chuck, and Nathan Bennett. "Big Data and Talent Management: Using Hard Data to Make the Soft Stuff Easy." *Business Horizons* 58, no. 3 (2015): 237–42. https://doi.org/10.1016/j.bushor.2014.08.001.

Salas, Eduardo, Scott I. Tannenbaum, Steve W. C. Kozlowski, Christopher A. Miller, John E. Mathieu, and William B. Vessey. "Teams in Space Exploration." *Current Directions in Psychological Science* 24, no. 3 (2015): 200–207. https://doi.org/10.1177/0963721414566448.

Tonidandel, Scott, Eden B. King, and Jose M. Cortina, eds. *Big Data at Work: The Data Science Revolution and Organizational Psychology.* New York: Routledge, 2016.

van Vulpen, Erik. "Top 5 Trending HR Analytics Articles of July 2017." *Analytics in HR* (blog), August 2017, www.analyticsinhr.com/blog/trending-hr-analytics-articles-august-2017/?utm_content=buffer3746a&utm_medium=social&utm_source=twitter.com&utm_campaign=buffer.

Waber, Ben. *People Analytics: How Social Sensing Technology Will Transform Business and What It Tells Us about the Future of Work.* Upper Saddle River, NJ: FT Press, 2013.

Analytics Talent Development
Competency-Based Skills

Society for Human Resource Management. *The SHRM Body of Competency and Knowledge.* Alexandria: Society for Human Resource Management, 2017. www.shrm.org/certification/Documents/SHRM-BoCK-FINAL.pdf.

Analytics Function Development

Creelman, David. "3 Mistakes to Avoid When Starting an HR Analytics Function." *Clarity*, June 2017. www.visier.com/clarity/3-mistakes-hr-analytics-function/.

Fleisher, Matthew. "Creating a Human Capital Analytics Function in a Multinational Organization." Society for Human Resource Management, August 21, 2017. www.shrm.org/hr-today/trends-and-forecasting/special-reports-and-expert-views/Pages/Matthew%20Fleisher.aspx.

Guenole, Nigel, Sheri Feinzig, Jonathan Ferrar, and Joanne Allden. *Starting the Workforce Analytics Journey: The First 100 Days.* IBM Analytics Executive Report. Somers, NY: IBM Corporation, 2015. http://www-01.ibm.com/common/ssi/cgi-bin/ssialias?subtype=WH&infotype=SA&htmlfid=LOL14045USEN&attachment=LOL14045USEN.PDF.

Kamp, Morten. "How You Create a Superhero Analytics Team." *All about Human Capital* (blog), February 6, 2014. www.mortenkamp.com/2014/06/02/how-you-create-a-superhero-analytics-team/.

IBM Watson Talent. "10 Steps to Workforce Analytics Success in the First 100 Days." YouTube, July 7, 2015. www.youtube.com/watch?v=zjSM0zJOC40.

Storytelling

Anderson, Chris. "How to Give a Killer Presentation." *Harvard Business Review*, June 2013. www.hbr.org/2013/06/how-to-give-a-killer-presentation.

Buchanan, Leigh. "Both Simple and True: The Secrets of Effective Storytelling." *Inc.*, October 2013. www.inc.com/magazine/201310/leigh-buchanan/the-moth-storytelling-secrets.html.

Stanton, Andrew. "The Clues to a Great Story." Presentation at TED2012, Long Beach, CA, February 28, 2012. www.ted.com/talks/andrew_stanton_the_clues_to_a_great_story?referrer=playlist-how_to_tell_a_story.

Data Visualization

Al-Kassab, Jasser, Zied M. Ouertani, Giovanni Schiuma, and Andy Neely. "Information Visualization to Support Management Decisions." *International Journal of Information Technology and Decision Making* 13, no. 2 (2013): 407–28. https://doi.org/10.1142/s0219622014500497.

Darling, Kayla. "Fifteen Cool Data Visualization Examples from 2016." *Visme* (blog), January 3, 2017. www.blog.visme.co/best-information-graphics-2016/.

Journalist's Resource. "Data Journalism Syllabus: From Numeracy to Visualization and Beyond." Last updated May 9, 2017. www.journalistsresource.org/syllabi/data-journalism-visualization-mapping-ethics-syllabus.

Gorodov, Evgeniy Yur'evich, and Vasiliy Vasil'evich Gubarev. "Analytical Review of Data Visualization Methods in Application to Big Data." *Journal of Electrical and Computer Engineering*, November 26, 2013. www.hindawi.com/journals/jece/2013/969458/.

Heer, Jeffrey, Michael Bostock, and Vadim Ogievetsky. "A Tour through the Visualization Zoo." *Communications of the ACM* 53, no. 6 (June 2010): 59–67. https://doi.org/10.1145/1743546.1743567.

McGhee, Geoff. "The 'Rules' of Data Visualization Get an Update." *National Geographic*, Data Points series, October 16, 2015. https://news.nationalgeographic.com/2015/10/151016-data-points-alberto-cairo-interview/.

Sinar, Evan F. "7 Data Visualization Types You Should Be Using More (and How to Start)." *Medium*, February 14, 2016. https://medium.com/@EvanSinar/7-data-visualization-types-you-should-be-using-more-and-how-to-start-4015b5d4adf2.

———. "Data Visualization." In Tonidandel, King, and Cortina, *Big Data at Work*, 115–57.

———. "DataViz Essentials: How Data Visualization Conquers Big Data's 4 Vs." LinkedIn Pulse, June 6, 2015. www.linkedin.com/pulse/dataviz-essentials-how-data-visualization-conquers-big-sinar-phd/.

———. "To Become a More Visionary Leader, Become Stronger at Visualization." *Medium*, May 29, 2016, https://medium.com/@EvanSinar/to-become-a-more-visionary-leader-become-stronger-at-visualization-4c629e133eb1.

———. "Use Animation to Supercharge Data Visualization." *Medium*, January 1, 2016. https://medium.com/@EvanSinar/use-animation-to-supercharge-data-visualization-cd905a882ad4.

Telea, Alexandru C. *Data Visualization: Principles and Practice*. 2nd ed. Boca Raton: CRC Press, 2015.

Wang, Lidong, Guanghui Wang, and Cheryl Ann Alexander. "Big Data and Visualization: Methods, Challenges and Technology Progress." *Digital Technologies* 1, no. 1 (2015): 33–38.

Data Collection/Research Methods

Beal, Daniel J. "ESM 2.0: State of the Art and Future Potential of Experience Sampling Methods in Organizational Research." *Annual Review of Organizational Psychology and Organizational Behavior* 2 (2015): 383–407. https://doi.org/10.1146/annurev-orgpsych-032414-111335.

Chaffin, Daniel, Ralph Heidl, John R. Hollenbeck, Michael Howe, Andrew Yu, Clay Voorhees, and Roger Calantone. "The Promise and Perils of Wearable Sensors in Organizational Research." *Organizational Research Methods* 20, no. 1 (2017): 3–31. https://doi.org/10.1177/1094428115617004.

Hernandez, Pedro. "Microsoft Workplace Analytics Lifts the Veil on Employee Productivity." *eWeek*, July 5, 2017. http://www.eweek.com/enterprise-apps/microsoft-workplace-analytics-lifts-the-veil-on-employee-productivity.

Kim, Taemie, Erin McFee, Daniel Olguin Olguin, Ben Waber, and Alex Pentland. "Sociometric Badges: Using Sensor Technology to Capture New Forms of Collaboration." *Journal of Organizational Behavior* 33, no. 3 (2012): 412–27. https://doi.org/10.1002/job.1776.

Landers, Richard N., Robert C. Brusso, Katelyn J. Cavanaugh, and Andrew B. Collmus. "A Primer on Theory-Driven Web Scraping: Automatic Extraction of Big Data from the Internet for Use in Psychological Research." *Psychological Methods* 21, no. 4 (2016): 475–92. https://doi.org/10.1037/met0000081.

Market Research Man. "Types of Data Measurement Scales: Nominal, Ordinal, Interval." *My Market Research Methods* (blog), March 31, 2017. www.mymarketresearchmethods.com/types-of-data-nominal-ordinal-interval-ratio/.

Pawlak-Dobrzánska, Marta. "Candidate Experience—What Is It and How to Survey It?" *Analytics in HR* (blog), June 12, 2017. www.analyticsinhr.com/blog/candidate-experience-survey/?utm_content=buffer9e21d&utm_medium=social&utm_source=twitter.com&utm_campaign=buffer.

Santoro, Jessica M., Aurora J. Dixon, Chu-Hsiang Chang, and Steve W. J. Kozlowski. "Measuring and Monitoring the Dynamics of Team Cohesion: Methods, Emerging Tools, and Advanced Technologies." In *Team Cohesion: Advances in Psychological Theory, Methods and Practice*, ed. Eduardo Salas, William B. Vessey, and Armando X. Estrada, Research on Managing Groups and Teams 17 (Bingley, Eng: Emerald Group Publishing Limited, 2015), 115–45. http://www.emeraldinsight.com/doi/abs/10.1108/S1534-085620150000017006.

Society for Human Resource Management. "Building a Market-Based Pay Structure from Scratch." January 12, 2018. www.shrm.org/resourcesandtools/tools-and-samples/toolkits/pages/buildingamarket-basedpaystructurefromscratch.aspx.

Statistics

Bosco, Frank A., Herman Aguinis, Kulraj Singh, James G. Field, and Charles A. Pierce. "Correlational Effect Size Benchmarks." *Journal of Applied Psychology* 100, no. 2 (2015): 431–49. https://doi.org/10.1037/a0038047.

"Descriptive Statistics." Excel Easy, 2018. http://www.excel-easy.com/examples/descriptive-statistics.html.

Gupta, Dishashree. "41 Questions on Statistics for Data Scientists & Analysts." *Analytics Vidhya* (blog), May 4, 2017. www.analyticsvidhya.com/blog/2017/05/41-questions-on-statisitics-data-scientists-analysts/.

Institute for Digital Research and Education. "Choosing the Correct Statistical Test in SAS, Stata, SPSS and R." University of California at Los Angeles, 2017. https://stats.idre.ucla.edu/other/mult-pkg/whatstat/.

Jackson, Shawna, Karen Marcus, Cara McDonald, Timothy Wehner, and Mike Palmquist. "Statistics: An Introduction." Colorado State University, 2012. https://writing.colostate.edu/guides/guide.cfm?guideid=67.

Kufs, Charlie. "The Right Tool for the Job." *Stats with Cats Blog*, August 27, 2010. www.statswithcats.wordpress.com/2010/08/27/the-right-tool-for-the-job/.

Menon, Pradeep. "Data Science Simplified Part 2: Key Concepts of Statistical Learning." *Data Science Central*, August 6, 2017. www.datasciencecentral.com/profiles/blogs/data-science-simplified-key-concepts-of-statistical-learning.

Office of Planning, Assessment, Research and Quality. "Quantitative Data Analysis: Choosing a Statistical Test." University of Wisconsin-Stout, December 4, 2015. http://wwwcs.uwstout.edu/parq/intranet/upload/what_quant_test_to_use.pdf.

Stangroom, Jeremy. "Which Statistical Test Should I Use?" Social Science Statistics, 2018. www.socscistatistics.com/tests/what_stats_test_wizard.aspx.

Stone, Dianna L., and Patrick J. Rosopa. "Using Meta-analysis to Enhance Our Understanding of Human Resource Management." *Human Resource Management Review* 27, no. 1 (2017): 1–7. https://doi.org/10.1016/j.hrmr.2016.09.001.

Trochim, William M. K. "Selecting Statistics." Social Research Methods, accessed February 8, 2018. www.socialresearchmethods.net/selstat/ssstart.htm.

Advanced Analytics Techniques

Aguinis, Herman, Lura E. Forcum, and Harry Joo. "Using Market Basket Analysis in Management Research." *Journal of Management* 39, no. 7 (2013): 1799–824. https://doi.org/10.1177/0149206312466147.

Al-Hassan, Abeer A., Faleh Alshameri, and Edgar H. Sibley. "A Research Case Study: Difficulties and Recommendations When Using a Textual Data Mining Tool." *Information and Management* 50, no. 7 (2013): 540–52. https://doi.org/10.1016/j.im.2013.05.010.

Bligh, Michelle C., and Jeffrey C. Kohles. "Comparing Leaders across Contexts, Culture, and Time: Computerized Content Analysis of Leader-Follower Communications." *Leadership* 10, no. 2 (2014): 142–59. https://doi.org/10.1177/1742715011434109.

Colley, Sarah K., and Andrew Neal. "Automated Text Analysis to Examine Qualitative Differences in Safety Schema among Upper Managers, Supervisors and Workers." *Safety Science* 50, no. 9 (2012): 1775–85. https://doi.org/10.1016/j.ssci.2012.04.006.

Collins, Judith M., and Murray R. Clark. "An Application of The Theory of Neural Computation to the Prediction of Workplace Behavior: An Illustration and Assessment of Network Analysis." *Personnel Psychology* 46, no. 3 (1993): 503–24. https://doi.org/10.1111/j.1744-6570.1993.tb00882.x.

Detienne, Kristen B., David H. Detienne, and Shirish A. Joshi. "Neural Networks as Statistical Tools for Business Researchers." *Organizational Research Methods* 6, no. 2 (2003): 236–65. https://doi.org/10.1177/1094428103251907.

Grand, James A., Michael T. Braun, Goran Kuljanin, Steve W. J. Kozlowski, and Georgia T. Chao. "The Dynamics of Team Cognition: A Process-Oriented Theory of Knowledge Emergence in Teams." *Journal of Applied Psychology* 101, no. 10 (2016): 1353–85. https://doi.org/10.1037/apl0000136.

Haak, Tom. "How Can Organisational Network Analysis Help in HR?" *Trends in HR* (blog), May 1, 2017. hrtrendinstitute.com/2017/05/01/organisational-network-analysis/.

Intrator, Orna, and Nathan Intrator. "Interpreting Neural-Network Results: A Simulation Study." *Computational Statistics and Data Analysis* 37, no. 3 (2001): 373–93. https://doi.org/10.1016/s0167-9473(01)00016-0.

James, Gareth, Daniela Witten, Trevor Hastie, and Robert Tibshirani. *An Introduction to Statistical Learning with Applications in R.* Springer Texts in Statistics 103. New York: Springer, 2013. http://www-bcf.usc.edu/~gareth/ISL/ISLR%20First%20Printing.pdf.

Janasik, Nina, Timo Honkela, and Henrik Bruun. "Text Mining in Qualitative Research: Application of an Unsupervised Learning Method." *Organizational Research Methods* 12, no. 3 (2008): 436–60. https://doi.org/10.1177/1094428108317202.

Kaplan, David, and Jianshen Chen. "Bayesian Model Averaging for Propensity Score Analysis." *Multivariate Behavioral Research* 49, no. 6 (2014): 505–17. https://doi.org/10.1080/00273171.2014.928492.

Karanika-Murray, Maria, and Tom Cox. "The Use of Artificial Neural Networks and Multiple Linear Regression in Modelling Work-Health Relationships: Translating Theory into Analytical Practice." *European Journal of Work and Organizational Psychology* 19, no. 4 (2010): 461–86. https://doi.org/10.1080/13594320902995916.

Kozlowski, Steve W. J. "Advancing Research on Team Process Dynamics: Theoretical, Methodological, and Measurement Considerations." *Organizational Psychology Review* 5, no. 4 (2015): 270–99. https://doi.org/10.1177/2041386614533586.

Kozlowski, Steve W. J., and Katherine J. Klein. "A Multilevel Approach to Theory and Research in Organizations: Contextual, Temporal, and Emergent Processes." In *Multilevel Theory, Research, and Methods in Organizations: Foundations, Extensions, and New Directions*, ed. Katherine J. Klein and Steve W. J. Kozlowski, 3–90. San Francisco: Jossey-Bass, 2000. www.researchgate.net/publication/232580888_A_multilevel_approach_to_theory_and_research_in_organizations_Contextual_temporal_and_emergent_processes.

Kozlowski, Steve W. J., Georgia T. Chao, James A. Grand, Michael T. Braun, and Goran Kuljanin. "Advancing Multilevel Research Design: Capturing the Dynamic of Emergence." *Organizational Research Methods* 16, no. 4 (2013): 581–615. https://doi.org/10.1177/1094428113493119.

———. "Capturing the Multilevel Dynamics of Emergence: Computational Monitoring, Simulation, and Virtual Experimentation." *Organizational Psychology Review* 6, no. 1 (2016): 3–33. https://doi.org/10.1177/2041386614547955.

Kuhn, Max, and Kjell Johnson. *Applied Predictive Modeling*. New York: Springer Science+Business Media, 2013.

Linoff, Gordon, and Michael J. A. Berry. *Data Mining Techniques: For Marketing, Sales, and Customer Relationship Management*. 3rd ed. Indianapolis: Wiley, 2012.

Marksberry, Phillip, Joshua Church, and Michael Schmidt. "The Employee Suggestion System: A New Approach Using Latent Semantic Analysis." *Human Factors and Ergonomics in Manufacturing & Service Industries* 24, no. 1 (2012): 29–39. https://doi.org/10.1002/hfm.20351.

McCracken, Nancy, Jasy Liew Suet Yan, and Kevin Crowston. "Design of an Active Learning System with Human Correction for Content Analysis." *Proceedings of the Workshop on Interactive Language Learning, Visualization, and Interfaces*, 59–62. Baltimore: Association for Computational Linguistics, 2014. https://doi.org/10.3115/v1/w14-3109.

McKee, Rob A., and C. C. Miller. "Institutionalizing Bayesianism Within the Organizational Sciences: A Practical Guide Featuring Comments from Eminent Scholars." *Journal of Management* 41, no. 2 (2014): 471–90. https://doi.org/10.1177/0149206314546750.

Minbashian, Amirali, Jim E. H. Bright, and Kevin D. Bird. "A Comparison of Artificial Neural Networks and Multiple Regression in the Context of Research on Personality and Work Performance." *Organizational Research Methods* 13, no. 3 (2009): 540–61. https://doi.org/10.1177/1094428109335658.

Nalbantian, Haig. "Navigating Human Capital Risk and Uncertainty Report." White paper. Mercer, June 30, 2017. www.mercer.com/our-thinking/career/voice-on-talent/navigating-human-capital-risk-and-uncertainty-report.html.

Paganoni, Anna M., and Piercesare Secchi, eds. *Advances in Complex Data Modeling and Computational Methods in Statistics*. Cham, Che.: Springer International, 2015.

Putka, Dan J., Adam S. Beatty, and Matthew C. Reeder. "Modern Prediction Methods: New Perspectives on a Common Problem." *Organizational Research Methods*, April 3, 2017. https://doi.org/10.1177/1094428117697041.

Rokach, Lior. "Ensemble-Based Classifiers." *Artificial Intelligence Review* 33, no. 1–2 (2010): 1–39. https://doi.org/10.1007/s10462-009-9124-7.

Schmidt-Atzert, Lothar, Stefan Krumm, and Dirk Lubbe. "Toward Stable Predictions of Apprentices' Training Success." *Journal of Personnel Psychology* 10, no. 1 (2011): 34–42. https://doi.org/10.1027/1866-5888/a000027.

Seni, Giovanni, and John F. Elder. *Ensemble Methods in Data Mining: Improving Accuracy through Combining Predictions*. Synthesis Lectures on Data Mining and Knowledge Discovery. San Rafael, CA: Morgan and Claypool, 2010.

Somers, Mark J. "Application of Two Neural Network Paradigms to the Study of Voluntary Employee Turnover." *Journal of Applied Psychology* 84, no. 2 (1999): 177–85. https://doi.org/10.1037/0021-9010.84.2.177.

———. "Thinking Differently: Assessing Nonlinearities in the Relationship between Work Attitudes and Job Performance Using a Bayesian Neural Network." *Journal of Occupational and Organizational Psychology* 74, no. 1 (2001): 47–61. https://doi.org/10.1348/096317901167226.

Somers, Mark J., and Jose C. Casal. "Using Artificial Neural Networks to Model Nonlinearity: The Case of the Job Satisfaction–Job Performance Relationship." *Organizational Research Methods* 12, no. 3 (2009): 403–17. https://doi.org/10.1177/1094428107309326.

Yamkovenko, Bogdan, and John P. Hatala. "Methods for Analysis of Social Networks Data in HRD Research." *Advances in Developing Human Resources* 17, no. 1 (2015): 40–56. https://doi.org/10.1177/1523422314559806.

Yan, Jasy Liew Suet, Nancy McCracken, and Kevin Crowston. "Semi-Automatic Content Analysis of Qualitative Data." *IConference 2014 Proceedings*, January 2014, 1128–32. https://doi.org/10.9776/14399.

Evidence-Based Practice
Barends, Eric, Denise M. Rousseau, and Rob B. Briner, eds. CEBMa Guideline for Critically Appraised Topics in Management and Organizations. Amsterdam: Center for Evidence-Based Management, 2017. www.cebma. org/wp-content/uploads/CEBMa-CAT-Guidelines.pdf.

Statistical Pitfalls
Dietvorst, Berkeley J. "When People Don't Trust Algorithms." Interview by Paul Michelman. *MIT Sloan Management Review*, Fall 2017. www.sloanreview. mit.edu/article/when-people-dont-trust-algorithms/.

Lambrecht, Anja, and Catherine Tucker. "The 4 Mistakes Most Managers Make with Analytics." *Harvard Business Review*, July 12, 2016. www.hbr. org/2016/07/the-4-mistakes-most-managers-make-with-analytics.

Louis, Winnifred, and Cassandra Chapman. "The Seven Deadly Sins of Statistical Misinterpretation, and How to Avoid Them." *The Conversation US*, March 28, 2017. www.theconversation.com/the-seven-deadly-sins-of-statistical-misinterpretation-and-how-to-avoid-them-74306?utm_source=facebook&utm_medium=facebookbutton.

Tools
van Vulpen, Erik. "Top 5 HR Analytics Tools." *Analytics in HR*, May 11, 2017. www.analyticsinhr.com/blog/hr-analytics-tools/.

General Tools
Amazon Web Services. "Amazon Machine Images (AMI)." 2018. https://docs. aws.amazon.com/AWSEC2/latest/UserGuide/AMIs.html.

IBM. "Build on the AI Platform for Business." Accessed December 23, 2018. www.ibm.com/watson/developer/.

"Deep Learning for Java." Skymind, accessed February 8, 2018. www. deeplearning4j.org/.

Hall, Mark, Eibe Frank, Geoffrey Holmes, Bernhard Pfahringer, Peter Reutermann, and Ian H. Witten. "The WEKA Data Mining Software: An Update." *ACM SIGKDD Explorations Newsletter* 11, no. 1 (2009): 10–18. https://doi.org/10.1145/1656274.1656278.

Hanson, J. Jeffery. "An Introduction to the Hadoop Distributed File System." DeveloperWorks, February 1, 2011. www.ibm.com/developerworks/library/wa-introhdfs/index.html.

KDnuggets. www.kdnuggets.com/.
Tableau Software. www.tableau.com/.
Revolutions (blog), Microsoft. http://blog.revolutionanalytics.com/.

Tutorials

Bird, Steven, Ewan Klein, and Edward Loper. "Language Processing and
   Python." In *Natural Language Processing with Python*, 1–34. Sebastopol, CA:
   O'Reilly Media, 2014. www.nltk.org/book/ch01.html.
Content Team. "A Complete Tutorial on Tree Based Modeling
   from Scratch (in R & Python)." *Analytics Vidhya* (blog),
   May 1, 2017. www.analyticsvidhya.com/blog/2016/04/
   complete-tutorial-tree-based-modeling-scratch-in-python/.
Husson, François. *Exploratory Multivariate Analysis with R and FactoMineR*.
   YouTube playlist, accessed February 8, 2018. www.youtube.com/playlist?list
   =PLnZgp6epRBbTsZEFXi_p6W48HhNyqwxIu&feature.
Murphy, Philip. *Basic Text Mining in R*. April 4, 2017. https://rpubs.com/
   pjmurphy/265713.
Neto, João. *Neural Networks*. May 2013. www.di.fc.ul.pt/~jpn/r/neuralnets/
   neuralnets.html.
Olson, Randy. "Data Visualization Basics with Python: Tips, Techniques, and
   Best Practices for Effective Chart Visualizations with matplotlib." Video
   training course. Infinite Skills, January 20, 2016. http://shop.oreilly.com/
   product/0636920046592.do.
"R Tutorials." ThinkToStart. www.thinktostart.com/category/
   datascience/r-tutorials/.
RDataMining.com: R and Data Mining. www.rdatamining.com/.
Spector, Phil. "Cluster Analysis." Notes for Statistics 133, Spring 2011. www.
   stat.berkeley.edu/~s133/Cluster2a.html.
"Tutorials." DataCamp. www.datacamp.com/community/tutorials.

Evidence-Based Practice Tutorials

EBSCO Help. "My EBSCOhost Folder - Tutorial." YouTube, October 30,
   2015. www.youtube.com/watch?v=bsnSAf5NYe8.
———. "Using the EBSCOhost Search History - Tutorial." YouTube,
   November 11, 2015. www.youtube.com/watch?v=cqiGklTi6CM.

Index